ANIMAL DRAUGHT TECHNOLOGY
An annotated bibliography

Jane Bartlett and David Gibbon

Practical Action Publishing Ltd
25 Albert Street, Rugby, CV21 2SD, Warwickshire, UK
www.practicalactionpublishing.com
in association with
Co-operative Educational Materials Advisory Service
of the International Co-operative Alliance

© Intermediate Technology Publications Ltd, 1984

First published in 1984
Transferred to digital printing in 2008

ISBN 13 Paperback: 9780946688319
ISBN Library Ebook: 9781780441900
Book DOI: https://doi.org/10.3362/9781780441900

All rights reserved. No part of this publication may be reprinted or reproduced or utilized in any form or by any electronic, mechanical, or other means, now known or hereafter invented, including photocopying and recording, or in any information storage or retrieval system, without the written permission of the publishers.

A catalogue record for this book is available from the British Library.

The authors, contributors and/or editors have asserted their rights under the Copyright Designs and Patents Act 1988 to be identified as authors of their respective contributions.

Since 1974, Practical Action Publishing has published and disseminated books and information in support of international development work throughout the world. Practical Action Publishing is a trading name of Practical Action Publishing Ltd (Company Reg. No. 01159018), the wholly owned publishing company of Practical Action. Practical Action Publishing trades only in support of its parent charity objectives and any profits are covenanted back to Practical Action (Charity Reg. No. 247257, Group VAT Registration No. 880 9924 76).

Reasonable efforts have been made to publish reliable data and information, but the author and publisher cannot assume responsibility for the validity of all materials or for the consequences of their use.

The manufacturer's authorised representative in the EU for product safety is Lightning Source France, 1 Av. Johannes Gutenberg, 78310 Maurepas, France. compliance@lightningsource.fr

CONTENTS

	Page
1. Introduction	1
2. Acknowledgements	2
3. Overview	
1. Choice of Technology	3
1. Policy Issues	3
2. Physical and Technical Issues	4
2. Situation Analysis - Impact, Adoption & Diffusion	6
3. The Technology of Animal Draught Use	8
1. Tillage Techniques, Implements and Harnessing	8
2. Draught Capacity, Training, Nutrition and General Management	10
4. Bibliography	
1. Choice of Technology	12
2. Situation Analysis	28
3. Technology of Animal Draught Use	42
3.1 Tillage Techniques, Implements and Harnessing	42
3.2 Draught Capacity, Training, Nutrition and General Management	59
4. General	73
5. Conclusion	75

Annexes

1. Organisations with an interest in promoting the use of draught animals

2. Index of bibliography items by country or region

3. Index of bibliography items by author or institution

1. INTRODUCTION

This study has been undertaken as part of a long term research interest in animal draught technologies within small farm systems by members of the School of Development Studies.

It was begun in response to the regular flow of enquiries to the School and Intermediate Technology Development Group from field workers and institutions in developing countries and from people in the UK intending to work overseas. Most of these people wished to have answers to a range of technical problems associated with the introduction of animal draught power into small farm systems and information on alternatives to existing equipment and technology.

The current focus and interest in the potential role and value of animal draught within small farm systems is not surprising in view of the length of time during which draught animals have been used in agriculture and also the wide range of situations in which animal draught still forms an integral part of farming systems. The inadequate performance and sustainability of tractor based mechanisation systems in many developing countries has further stimulated interest in a re-examination of animal draught as a major power source for many of the developing world's poorer farmers.

The objectives of this study are:

1) To review literature concerned with the factors affecting the choice of technology both at the national level and at the level of individual or groups of farmers with limited resources.

2) To examine a number of contrasting case studies that may indicate the reason for limited or widespread adoption of animal draught technologies.

3) To examine the technology of animal draught use with an emphasis on the need to explore the alternatives to present methods.

4) To review the state of knowledge on animal power and its efficiency and management in farming.

The review is restricted in a number of ways - mostly to work in anglophone countries, predominantly in Africa and Asia, and is highly selective, a sample only of key or available references have been examined. Fuller bibliographies are under way by other workers in this field.

The overall purpose of the work is to provide some practical summary of current knowledge that will be of value to field workers and students of animal draught.

The following overview discusses the key concepts under each major area of interest, and the subsequent bibliography is organised under the same broad headings.

ACKNOWLEDGEMENTS

This work inevitably draws on the studies and work of many people. An earlier bibliography of Simon Bell, the studies of Michael Goe, Dr. N.S. Ramaswamy, Peter Munzinger and the work of a series of Development Studies Students have all made significant contributions.

We have also benefitted from helpful comments from Frank Inns, Stephen Biggs and Michael Goe on an earlier draft.

3.   OVERVIEW

1. **Choice of Technology**

Though we are primarily concerned with animal draught technology in small farm systems, it needs to be recognised at the outset that it is usually not possible to specify the form that technology should take in any situation; choices may not be clear cut and in practice, combinations of power sources, equipment and other inputs make up the complete technology mix.

We consider that it is necessary to examine the basic factors that are known to influence the choice of production technology and it is generally held that they fall into two broad groups; firstly, the political and economic policies of governments that affect the economic environment at farm level and, secondly, the technical efficiency of power sources and equipment that affect productivity of crops, labour and other resources.

1.1 **Policy issues**

Governments of developing countries often adopt agricultural policies that are intended to stimulate the production of sufficient food, fibre and industrial crops to provide for internal needs and for export. At the same time governments wish to spread the benefits of any wealth generated in agriculture through greater access to resources (land and also inputs) and the creation of greater employment opportunities with agriculture or in service and support industries.

In attempting to implement these policies many governments have failed to achieve their goals due to a variety of reasons, in some cases because the initial choice of the production technology mix was inappropriate and in others due to the effects of economic factors outside the direct control of either governments or individual farmers.

Undoubtedly, the evolution of technology in many Western countries during the last 60 years has had a profound effect on the thinking of developing country policy makers. More capital intensive farming methods involving the replacement of hand and animal powered systems by mechanical devices, have been introduced in many areas. The introduction of the tractor, and its associated Western developed equipment, has been seen as an essential step in the modernisation process and many governments have encouraged farmers or groups to purchase or hire equipment at favourable prices. Such policies have had different effects in different areas (see next section), but in general they have led to the devaluing of animals as a power source, the displacement of labour (particularly where wage rates are high) and the increase of larger farms at the expense of small farms.

It is now generally accepted that much of the technology that has been imported into developing countries is too complex for the available skills and maintenance infrastructures in most developing countries. Initial cost is frequently high and there is a high dependence on a continuing supply of external inputs.

It would appear that the initial analyses that gave rise to these policies were often inadequate or in their implementation the levels of pricing of inputs and outputs that may have facilitated widespread adoption of and benefits from the new technologies were incorrect.

Some economic analyses that could be of value in planning follow a short term approach using cost benefit analyses and optimising models such as linear programming. These typically compare the costs and returns of the different technologies, which costs worked out on an 'owned' or 'hired' basis. On this microeconomic level it would seem that oxen cultivation is superior to tractor based cultivation in terms of economic efficiency in most areas, while at the macroeconomic level it is generally held that in the medium and long term animal traction will be less of a burden on a countries balance of payments than a tractor based technology which has the largest foreign exchange requirement of all levels of agricultural mechanisation.

It has been suggested that an evaluation of the employment criteria be obtained through a scale which rates as most appropriate that technology which creates the most new jobs and least appropriate that which eliminates most jobs, with a neutral effect on job numbers being the threshold of acceptability, since any displaced (practically unskilled) labour from the rural areas in most developing nations will not be able to be absorbed into the industrial sector where job opportunities may be limited (Kinsey 1980). Studies on the effect of technology innovations on employment indicate that large scale tractorisation programmes displace up to half the agricultural labour engaged in bullock farming, although the issue is a complex one and effects will depend largely on the local situation (see next section).

Other discussions on the choice of technology argue the case for draught animal technology based on the availability of animals as a local renewable source of energy; the versatility of animals within the farming system; the relatively lower level of skills required for use and maintenance; the greater growth linkages with other sectors of the rural economy and the differences between private and social benefits of each technology type (Abeyratne <1982>; Ahmed <1977>; Beeny <1975>; Bose, Clark <1969>; Haswell <1979>; Johnson <1981>; Lele <1975>).

1.2 Physical and technical issues

Farm level technical issues feature predominantly in the literature. The rationale for moving to some form of mechanisation, tractor or animal draught based, is often to increase the area that can be cultivated, or the timeliness or quality of operations using the same amount of labour. Issues relating to the displacement or increase in productivity of labour are often confused with those involving changes in quality of work.

While it is possible to determine appropriate 'command' areas for hand, animal powered and tractor powered systems (Baker 1981) thus implying a close relationship between farm size and farm equipment and power and economics of scale, all motive power systems can be managed on a group or cooperative basis or other arrangements are feasible.

Some recent literature discusses the tractor v. animal draught debate at length but much is made of comparative performance studies under rather constrained or controlled conditions, and few consider the importance of potential for service or custom work both inside and outside agriculture which can determine the viability of any mechanisation system.

Adelhelm, Schmidt (1975); Agarwal (1978); Ahmed (1979); Binswanger, Ghodake and Thierstein (1979); Dunham (1979); Ker (1973); Munzinger (1982); Starkey, Verhaeghe (1982); Stokes (1963).

There appears to be very little evidence of crop yield differences between systems using tractor or animal power. Clearly, the introduction of either allows larger areas to be cultivated, and this usually results in an increase in farm production, but yields per unit area are either not affected or decline with the introduction of mechanisation. The exception to this general finding is on soils that benefit from an initial or periodic opening up with the additional power provided by animals or tractors.

More useful empirical studies of all the issues surrounding the oxen/tractor debate take a 'systems' approach to the subject (Collinson (1977); Muchiri/Minto (1977)) rather than the more narrowbased studies concentrating on analyses of single crops or operations. The precise difficulty in the choice of technology is that none of the combinations of technology have all beneficial or all detrimental consequences; most produce a mixture of effects. Technology choice should logically be appraised in the context of the farming system within which it is proposed to apply it. For this kind of appraisal it is therefore essential to evaluate concurrently all the factors affecting production in any specific area. Among the literature are several detailed studies of specific agro-ecological and socio-economic environments dealing with the impact of technological innovations on production, incomes and employment. In the light of their results these studies are able to propose useful guidelines for future policies regarding the development of farm power, the concensus of opinion being that productive and profitable farming systems are possible using animals traction as the main power source.

Abeyratne (1982); Bakler, White (1983); Farrington, Abeyratne (1982); Finney (1972); Gill (1981); Jabbar (1980); Kinsey (1980, 1981 a + b); Pollard, Wainaina (1982); Rryan, Abeyratne, Farrington (1982); Singh, Subramanium (1977).

The potential benefits of draught animals as a provider of manure and fuel are also worthy of note but rarely accounted for in mechanical/animal comparisons.

Situational Analysis - Impact, Adoption and Diffusion

Although the use of draught animal power (DAP) is widespread throughout the developing world there are considerable differences in situation between Asia, Africa and Latin America, and also between countries in each of these areas. Over much of Asia (India, Sri Lanka, Bangladesh, Pakistan, China) and in some Northern African countries (particularly Egypt and Ethiopia) DAP constitutes a major traditional source of energy, with well developed adaptations of tools and techniques and widespread use of animals, mainly bovine. It has been estimated that over half the power in agriculture in China and two thirds in India is supplied by draught animals (Ramaswamy 1981). In contrast to these areas, much of Africa has only recently seen the introduction of cultivation techniques using animals. The transition from hand hoes to draught animals has been sporadic and uneven, although in recent years there has been an increase in the initiation of oxenisation programmes as major components of national development policies. In Latin America the use of DAP, previously a strong traditional source of energy, has declined in favour of agricultural mechanisation policies involving tractors introduced into some areas as early as the 1950s. Some Latin American countries have shown interest in the revival of DAP following the fuel price rises and adverse effects of indiscriminate tractorisation, but no clear cut policies to favour DAP development seem to be in evidence. Nevertheless, several species of draught animals remain in use in parts of the continent for agricultural operations, transport and logging.

A summary of some characteristics with respect to animal draught in different regions is given in Table 1.

TABLE 1

		Types of animals	Relative importance as power source	Types of land use	Labour availability	Local skills, knowledge and experience with ADT	Energy provided by ADP/ powered mechanisation (ratio)	Limitations on animal use	Potential for expansion in ADT use
Africa [1]	N & E	Donkeys Oxen Horses Camels	High	mod. int. (N)	Low	High	5:1	Fodder	Low
	C & S	Oxen Donkeys	High	mod. int.	Moderate	Medium	5:1	Fodder Equipment Disease Service Markets	High
	W	Oxen Camels Donkeys	Low	mod. int.	Moderate	Medium	5:1	Disease Equipment Fodder Credit	High
Asia	S & E	Buffalo Oxen	High	very int.	High	High	80:1	Fodder	Low
	C & S	Oxen Buffalo Yaks	High	very int.	High	High	80:1	Fodder	Low
	W	Oxen Donkeys Camels	Low	mod. int.	Low	Medium	8:1	Labour Alt. power	Low
America	C	Oxen Horses Donkeys	Medium	mod. int.	Low	Medium	3:1	Alt. power Equipment Harness Credit	Mod.
	S	Oxen Horses Llamas	Medium	mod. ext.	Moderate	Medium	8:1	Fodder Equipment Harness Credit	Mod.

1 For greater detail on African countries see Munzinger, P. (1982).

Within these broad regional zones there are important differences, particularly in the numbers of animals available, the potential productivity of agro-ecological zones, person/land ratios and the availability of labour for draught animal work.

Much of the literature relevant to small farm animal technology documents the development and use of animals in different areas and countries, with descriptions and discussions of present systems and proposed projects.

An examination of animal traction projects in W, C & S Africa reveals the most common constraints to the adoption and effective use of animal draught technology as; technological deficiencies in prototype equipment, availability of land for farm expansion, competing labour demands, dry season animal maintenance, and inadequacy of support services, a major cause of low adoption rates especially with regard to credit availability.

Baker (1981); Barrett et al (1982); Fulton and Tomlinson (1982); Hang and Gerner-Hang (1982); ILCA (1981); Kjaerby (1983); Mettrick (1978); Munzinger (1982); Newhauser (1977); Okai (1978); Samson et al (1975); Sargent et al (1981); Sinid (1982); Starkey (1981); Tran van Nhien (1982); Uzurean (1974); Wagner and Munzinger (1982).

It can be concluded that the reasons for the varied adoption rate of animal draught and appropriate equipment is due to the varied mix of factors present in any one situation so it is difficult and perhaps dangerous to make any broad generalisations from this brief survey of literature In the concluding section an attempt is made to identify a set of criteria that may assist in the planning of microlevel research and development programmes and also provide a basis for policy formulation in areas relating to animal draught technology.

3. **The Technology of Animal Draught Use**

This section of the bibliography focuses on the technical aspects of draught animal use within small farm systems. Here we are concerned with the efficiency of soil, water and crop management using an appropriate range of equipment and tools and the ways in which optimum use can be made of draught animals within a farming system.

3.1 **Tillage techniques, implements and harnessing**

The design of efficient animal drawn implements depends to a large extent on the tillage technique practised in any farming system. The research and development efforts on appropriate tillage for tropical agricultural systems are widely covered in the literature, but, coverage of this aspect is beyond the scope of this bibliography. However, a brief discussion of the general direction of research into tillage techniques may help to introduce some perspective into the studies of equipment design included here.

Mouldboard ploughing, developed in temperate climates, has frequently proved inappropriate on many tropical soils, where it can aggravate runoff and soil erosion in heavy rainfall areas and increase evaporation of soil moisture in semi arid areas, also promoting loss of essential organic matter. In addition, the energy requirements for ploughing are very high in semi arid areas where the soil is often hard and dense at the start of the rainy season when cultivation and planting should occur. This period also coincides with the time of year when oxen are at their weakest with the quantity and quality of feed at its lowest. Therefore, systems of 'reduced or minimum tillage' are considered to be more appropriate for different agro-ecological zones with the following general objectives:

a) To reduce the energy input overall in cultivation, thereby conserving calorific requirements for both humans and animals and reducing labour demands, permitting faster land preparation and better timeliness in planting.

b) To reduce soil disturbance, thereby reducing erosion risk and evaporation and increasing infiltration.

c) To reduce weed growth (this is possible through systems of reduced tillage, although the main objective of mouldboard ploughing is often to reduce weed growth).

These objectives may also be achieved in some cases using herbicides, used solely or in combination with mechanical methods. It is considered, however, that the case for widespread use of herbicides in small farm systems has yet to be proven.

To complement new and existing tillage systems in different areas the design and production of improved animal drawn implements has increased in recent years. Much of the literature concerns the development, evaluation and technical specifications of the equipment, which cover all agricultural operations, land levelling, seedbed preparation, planting, weeding, harvesting and transport.

Barton, Jeanrenaud and Gibbon (1982); Boyd (1976a); Boyd, Ayok (1974) Brumby, Singh (1981); Chalmers, Marsden (1962); Cham (1979a); EFSAIP (1977, 1979-80); Fischer (1982); Foster (1980); Gibbon (1974); Gibbon, Harvey Hubbard (1974); Gibbon, Heslop, Harvey (1978); Kemp (1980); Khepar et al (1982); Matthews, Pullen (1977); Mochudi Farmers Brigade (1975); Muchiri (1979); Musa (1979); Ogborn (1979); Pathak (1982); Scott (1979); Willcocks (1969).

Results of trials undertaken to compare traditional and improved implements are presented in many studies, with manuals also published simply listing available equipment, locally produced and imported, in different areas.

Ali, Patra and Lall (1979); Boyd (1976b); Ellman, Mackay and Moody (1981); Matthews, Pullen (1976).

Much of the emphasis in recent years has been on the development of animal drawn tool carriers of varying complexity, which are designed to carry all the implements necessary for the main crop production operations. Currently, many workers favour single operation tools of strength and extreme simplicity with the greatest emphasis on land preparation and weeding operations. Some attention is also given to the possibilities and importance of utilising local resources and skills in the production of the equipment, thereby increasing availability, reducing costs and reducing dependence on imported products.

Although a considerable amount of work has been undertaken on the improvement of animal drawn implements, significantly less can be found dealing with the principles of and improvements to the harnessing of animals.

Barwell, Ayre (1982); Froese (1980); Hussain et al (1980); Varshney (1982); Viebig (1982).

Types of harness have an influence on the useful power output of the animals and hence on the working efficiency of the animal/equipment complex. Studies available on harnessing generally conclude that traditional yoke systems are relatively inefficient in transmitting the work output of the animal to the implement, and may also be harmful to the animal, causing a reduction to their useful working life. However, one problem that arises with an alternative system (such as padded collars) is that they are generally more expensive to produce than the traditional basic wooden yoke. Sound harnessing principles discussed in the literature relate to several criteria such as low cost, possibilities for local manufacture, easy maintenance and technical aspect covering fit, line of traction, attachment points and flexibility of movement.

3.2 **Draught capacity, training, nutrition and general management**

The draught work which must be carried out is determined on the basis of conditions relating to the farming system and economic factors, but the available tractive effort of the animal is a function of various factors relating to the animals themselves, the environment and aspects of management and husbandry.

Criteria relating to the animal such as species, breed, weight, age, sex and speed are of considerable importance. Several studies have been undertaken to determine the approximate draught capacity of different species and breeds of animals, with values obtained from trials carried out under local working conditions.

Buhle (1934); Devadattum, Maurya (1978); Goe and McDowell (1980); Ilangantileke et al (1980); Mukherjee et al (1961); Roy et al (1972); Smith (1979).

These also detail methods of measurement of draught and discuss the underlying draught principles. The results of trials are essential for the evaluation of the conformation and performance of local draught animals and for defining

possibilities for improvement in breeding for more efficient
animals. The question of the use of cows for work is also
of interest, with problems of balancing work and milk
production. Although comparatively few studies exist on
this aspect, the general opinion seems to be that with
careful management much could be gained from using cows
rather than bullocks for work in some areas.

Whilst improvement in the working efficiency of animals
begins with the selection of the animal, other management
factors have an important effect on work output. The method
of training and guidance of single animals or of teams of
animals has a significant influence on the quality of work
and the ease with which it is accomplished, since where
accurate work is required (for example interrow weeding or
on small plots) more control must be exercised over the
animals. In areas with no tradition of draught animal use,
adequate training and extension programmes will be needed to
devise ways of adapting existing animals to draught work or
to introduce appropriate draught species to the area, and
also to undertake the instruction of farmers in their use.

Information in the literature covers basic aspects of
training such as the use of reins, training yokes, nose
rings, harnesses, commands and training programmes, with
some discussion of the efficiency of the different methods
used, although this aspect of management is rather sparsely
covered compared with others.

Achiya and Udundo (1975); Barton, Jeanrenaud and Gibbon
(1982); Hall (undated).

A major constraint on animal work output is inadequate
nutrition. Frequently, as in the drier parts of Africa,
animals are maintained only on rough, often poorly managed,
grazing and consequently are in the worst possible condition
when they are most needed for work at the beginning of the
rainy season. Inadequate feeding practices for draught
animals stem from a variety of causes; farmers may not be
able to use labour to collect and conserve feedstuff or
maintain grazing due to other demands on labour time, or
they may not consider that the return is worthwhile, there
may be competition between human and animal needs, the
farmer may not be aware of the potential benefits of
adequate nutrition or of the value of local feedstuffs such
as crop residues, or there may be a shortage of cash for
purchasing additional feed if necessary. A general lack of
knowledge of nutritional requirements in others involved and
the consequent underestimation of the need for appropriate
feeding during the planning and implementation of projects
may also result in badly maintained and weak animals.
Undoubtedly more might be achieved if more attention were
given to nutritional requirements, but despite the
widespread use of animals comparatively little research has
been undertaken on this aspect. Some approximate figures
are available on the requirements of animals based on the
weight of the animal and the amount and type of work
undertaken, but few studies for specific areas are to be
found.

4. BIBLIOGRAPHY

4.1 Choice of Technology

1.1 ABEYRATNE, F. **Changing patterns of Farm Technology in Sri Lanka.** Paper presented at Regional Seminar on Farm Power, 25 - 29 October 1982, Agrarian Research and Training Institute, Colombo, SRI LANKA. (A.R.T.I., Colombo)

Analysis shows a massive transfer of technology in terms of using mechanical draught power. Changes in technology from animal to mechanical draught have become a serious burden to the national economy in terms of draining valuable foreign exchange in the import of tractors, spares and fuel. This has also had serious implications for the distribution of wealth, where most of it has accrued to the tractor owners. The changes have also had effects on employment through the displacement of labour. All factors point to the need for more rational planning with a shift back to the use of animal power.

1.2 ADELHELM, R; SCHMIDT, H. **Economic Aspects of Ox Cultivation.** in Proceedings of a Workshop on Farm Equipment Innovations for Agricultural Development and Rural Industrialisation, Occasional paper No. 16 (1975), Institute of Development Studies, University of Nairobi, KENYA. (Economic Planning Division and Land and Farm Management Division, Kenya Ministry of Agriculture.)

Economic analysis of different types of seedbed cultivation comparing ox, hand and tractor cultivation. Looks at limitations of cost comparison approach. Attempts to show appropriateness of technologies for different farm sizes. 8 - 10 hectare holdings use hand cultivation as long as the labour needs can be met by the family. On the larger farms oxen vs tractors depends on the intensity of cultivation which determines the opportunity cost of the land that would be used to graze oxen.

1.3 AGARWAL, B. **Agricultural mechanisation and Labour Use: A Disaggregated Approach.** Institute of Development Studies, Sussex, ENGLAND. (1979)

Operational breakup of employment effects of tractors. Found that tractors reduce labour in ploughing and sowing. The main displacement effect is on male labour.

SEE ALSO: Effect of Agricultural Mechanisation on Crop Output Institute of Development Studies, Sussex. (1979)

Paper finds little economic reason for tractors to have preference over bullocks.

1.4 AHMAD, B. **Bullock Farming Vs. Tractor Farming.** Agricultural Mechanisation in Asia (1979) 10 (3) : 51 - 54. (Department of Farm Management, University of Agriculture, Faisalabad, PAKISTAN.)

Study indicates the real impact on yields, costs, gross and net benefits to the cultivator on tractor and bullock farms. The conclusions drawn are; a) That land use was particularly of the same magnitude under bullock and mechanical cultivation. b) Mechanical farms employed a better cropping pattern than bullock farms. c) Tractor cultivation was more productive as it increased wheat yield by 13.8%, cotton by 1.8% and sugar cane by 13.0% more than that obtainable under bullock cultivation. d) Gross income per acre was higher on tractor farms by only 1.4%. e) Farm expenditures were less on tractor farms by about 5.7% and net income was higher by 27.5%. f) Roughly one third of the labour force engaged on bullock farms was displaced with the introduction of the tractors. This may act as a deterrent to mechanical cultivation especially where no alternative employment opportunities exist. Several policy suggestions are made in the light of these conclusions.

1.5 AHMED, I. **Appropriate Rice Production Technology for Bangladesh.** Paper presented at an International Conference on Rural Development Technology (1977), Asian Institute of Technology, Bangkok, THAILAND.

Evaluates biochemical technologies, power sources and combinations of biochemical with bullock and tractor power. Focus on unemployment. Concludes that high yielding varieties need more labour, and bullocks need more labour although they increase output over tractors.

1.6 BAKER, P. R.; WHITE, P. **An Evaluation of Policy Toward Agricultural Technology Choice for Power in Zambia.** Discussion Paper No. 121 February 1983, School of Development Studies, University of East Anglia, Norwich ENGLAND.

Discussion of the political history and economic structure of Zambia, focusing on the present technology policy favouring grossly inefficient, heavily subsidised emergent tractor farmer. Sets out to show how a mixed technology option based on a policy putting mechanical draught farming onto a more profitable basis (by equating it with an appropriate scale and efficiency of operation) and introducing widespread ox ownership for cultivation could be economically more efficient and also politically acceptable.

1.7 BARKER, R.; JOHNSON, S. S.; ALVIAR, N.; ORCIONO, N. **Comparative Economic Analysis of Farm Data on the use of Carabao and Tractors in Lowland Rice Farming.** Paper presented for the Farm Management Seminar sponsored by the Institute of Small Scale Industries, Manila, Philippines, 24 February - 1 March 1969.

1.8 BAUTISTA, F. E.; WICKHAM, T. **The Tractor and the Carabao: A Socioeconomic Study of Choice of Power Source for Land Preparation in Nueva Ecija.** F.A.O. Farm Management Notes No. 6 January 1979.

1.9 BEENY, J. M. **Agricultural Mechanisation Study.** Food and Agriculture Organisation (F.A.O.) Publication (1975)

Depicts existing "chaotic" situation in agricultural mechanisation. Economics and farm management are used as guides to appropriate forms of mechanisation. Small farms - bullocks, large farms - power equipment. Proposes agromechanisation centres for training, demonstration etc. and stimulation for village level oxen equipment production.

1.10 BINSWANGER, H. P.; GHODAKE, R. D. ; THIERSTEIN, G. E. **Observations on the Economics of Tractors, Bullocks and Wheeled Toolcarriers in the Semi-Arid Tropics of India.** in Proceedings, International Workshop on Socioeconomic Constraints to Development of Semi Arid Tropical Agriculture, Hyderabad, India 19 - 23 February 1979. International Crops Research Institute for the Semi Arid Tropics (I.C.R.I.S.A.T), INDIA.

Reviews the available survey evidence on the economics of tractor cultivation for the semi arid tropics of India. Found that tractor cultivation as generally practised does not improve cropping intensity or yields and displaces labour. This provides a justification for the emphasis on bullock power in the farming systems research programme. Evidence available on the economics of wheeled tool carriers is reviewed. Such machines cannot compete on a cost basis with traditional implements in traditional agriculture. They must provide yield advantages in the order of 200 - 400 kg/hectare to justify higher costs. Experimental station evidence suggests that this can be achieved, but such evidence is not yet available at the farmers field level. The critical issue for farm level adoption is the cost of the equipment and the market for service or cooperative use.

1.11 BOSE, S. R.; CLARK, E. H. **Some Basic Considerations on Agricultural Mechanisation in West Pakistan.** Pakistan Development Review (1969) 9 (3) ; 273 - 308.

Deals with social acceptability of mechanisation.
a) Direct benefits of mechanisation, increased yields/hectare, removes need to feed animals, increases timeliness. b) Direct costs of mechanisation, annual costs are greater than benefits. c) Indirect social cost, resettlement, meat, local industry. d) Indirect benefits, create mechanical skills, increase savings.
Concluded that private benefits are greater than social benefits.

SEE ALSO: **The Cost of Draught Animal Power in West Pakistan.** in Pakistan Development Review (1970) 10

Before the cost advantage/disadvantage of mechanical power over animal power can be calculated a definition of the costs and how they should be measured is necessary. Fixed and variable costs for mechanical implements are known, the problem arises with analysing the costs of animal power. Paper looks at the two methods generally used in the literature, contending that neither method is appropriate, and presents an appropriate concept of the social cost of DAP based on the structure of the animal population required to support one working animal and its fodder requirements, the total social cost per livestock unit set against the social benefits derived from the animals. (Hides, meat, bones, horns, hooves, manure, milk.) The advantage of the method (the results of which are roughly approximate to those obtained from the more traditional calculations) is that it allows direct computation of the cost reductions which would result from such improvements as longer life span, earlier working age etc. Several qualifications regarding the computations are made. Concludes by stating that economic justification of a policy of agricultural mechanisation must be based on the net social advantages and not on the direct cost advantages of mechanisation over animal power. (Especial attention should be given to social cost of displacing labour by tractors.)

1.12 BOSHOFF, W. H.; MINTO, S. D. **Energy Requirements and Labour Bottlenecks and their Influence on the Choice of Improved Equipment.** in Proceedings of a Workshop on Farm Equipment Innovations for Agricultural Development and Rural Industrialisation, Occasional Paper No. 16 (1975), Institute of Development Studies, University of Nairobi, KENYA.

Identifies and discusses labour bottlenecks and energy requirements in traditional farming operations. The easing of primary cultivation (singled out as the greatest labour consumer) with mechanisation (oxen or tractors) encourages increases in acreage. Consequently planting, weeding and harvesting, previously secondary bottlenecks become major constraints to productivity of the increased acreage. Therefore need to consider operations in farming cycle as a whole. Recommends greater use of multipurpose animal drawn equipment to overcome the problem.

1.13 BOYD, J. E. L. **Choice of Technology for Agricultural Development - Farm Machinery.** Paper presented at 4th UK Conference, Ghana Association for Development Studies. (Intermediate Technology Development Group).

Looks at potential benefits of farm mechanisation. (Technically better work, faster, less labour, ease of work), factors affecting the choice of technology (costs, maintenance, farm details, skills, labour availability, diseases, political aims) and compares different levels of technology in farm mechanisation. (Hand tools, oxen, small 2 wheel tractor and large 4 wheel tractor.)

1.14 CARR, M. **Animals and Tractors in Sri Lanka: A Case Study of Choice of Technique in Agriculture.** In 'Livestock in Less Developed Countries.' (ed) M. Lipton.

1.15 CASTILLO, L. S. **From Primative to Modern with Water Buffaloes.** Paper presented at an International Agriculture Development Seminar, Cornell University, Ithaca, New York, May 24 1967.

1.16 COLLINSON, M. P. **Diagnosing the Need for New Technolgy.** in Report of the Rural Technology Meet for East, Central and Southern Africa, Arusha, TANZANIA, 1977. Commonwealth Secretariat.

Emphasises that appropriateness of a particular implement can only be judged in the light of a particular local situation. The land/labour ratio, the nature of the farming system, availability of off-farm employment and the political objectives of the government are crucial factors determining the kind of technology which may be appropriate. Also vital to examine demand as well as supply. Advocates 'system thinking' as the key to identification of a need for new equipment.

1.17 DENNISON, J. V. **Buffaloes Vs. Tractors. A Comparison of their use in Village Agriculture in N. Thailand.** Paper presented at a Departmental Seminar on Rural Sociology, Cornell University, Ithaca, New York, October 1978.

1.18 DIXIT, R. S. **Pattern of Bullock Labour Employment on Aligarh Farms.** Agricultural Situation in India (1969) 23 (12); 1257 - 1263. (Department of Agricultural Economics, Banaras Hindu University, India.)

Report on a study of employment of bullock labour in agriculture - cropwise, operationwise and monthwise employment and relation of bullock labour input to total input and income.

1.19 DUNHAM, R. J. **Cultivation Experiments with Zero Tillage at I.A.R.; Zaria.** in Proceedings of the Appropriate Tillage Workshop, Institute of Agricultural Research (I.A.R), Zaria, Nigeria, 16 - 20 January 1979. Commonwealth Secretariat. (Department of Soil Science, I.A.R., Zaria, Nigeria.)

Comparisons of different cultivation systems on maize. Zero tillage, manual, bullock powered and tractor powered. Preliminary results indicate that little difference to the final yield between manual, bullock and tractor powered systems, with zero tillage found to be distinctly inferior.

1.20 FARRINGTON, J., ABEYRATNE, F. **The Impact of Small Farm Mechanisation in Sri Lanka.** Paper presented at the International Seminar on Farm Power, 25 - 29 October 1982, Agrarian Research and Training Institute, Colombo, SRI LANKA.

Survey focussing on the impact of small farm tractorisation in Sri Lanka. Data used from farms owning 4 wheel tractors, 2 wheel tractors, and buffalo, and from non-owning farms. Discussion of the effect of tractorisation on agricultural production, labour, the distribution of income and wealth and the social costs and benefits. Concludes that a limited role for tractors exists, but with higher use intensities (as opposed to direct substitution of animals) and a smaller tractor fleet than at present. For the bulk of tillage operations in which tractors are currently involved a (socially) less expensive and more equitable alternative exists in the broadbased ownership of small herds of draught animals.

1.21 FARRINGTON, J., ABEYRATNE, R., RYAN, M. J., BANDARA, J., **Draught Power for Small Farmers. A Critique of Planning Methodologies in Sri Lanka.** Journal of Agrarian Studies, Colombo, 1 (2) : 13 - 28 1980.

1.22 FINNEY, C. E. **The Economics of Farm Power in the Indus Plains of West Pakistan.** M.Phil Thesis, 1972, Univeristy of Reading, ENGLAND.

Models of typical farm conditions are presented and the effects of changing farm power inputs examined using linear programming with a computer. Five farm power situations are investigated;

a) The traditional system with traditional bullock power implements.
b) The introduction of mechanised wheat threshing to this system.
c) The use of improved bullock drawn implements.
d) Mechanised wheat thresing with improved implements.
e) Replacement of bullocks with tractor cultivation.

Each system is examined under four separate conditions of holding size and land tenure. Analyses are made of the expected economic returns to different farm power improvements. Effects on employment are considered and returns from other farm inputs compared.
Concludes that the introduction of tractor cultivation would not be economically justified on small and medium irrigated farms. On larger farms replacement of sharecropping tenants and bullocks by tractor cultivation would be highly profitable to the landowner, but from the point of view of national economy would not be justified due to massive labour displacement and unemployment. There is scope for the improvement of traditional bullock power systems on all farm sizes. Policy recommendations based on the conclusions drawn are discussed.

1.23 FRIGGINS, A. R., WALLIS, M. **Alice and the Two Bullocks of the Apocalypse.** Undergraduate Dissertation (1969), School of Development Studies, University of East Anglia, Norwich, ENGLAND.

Discussion of current heavy dependence of U.K. agriculture on non-renewable energy resources. Description of the technical aspects of a possible alternative sourceof energy (bullock power) to meet the draught power requirements in U.K. agriculture with an interpretation of statistics regarding potential land use patterns and how these relate to meeting the recommended food requirements of both humans and bovines in the context of a farm system based on the use of DAP. Concludes with a discussion of the implications of the proposed alternative system with regard to planning, politics and philosophy in the agricultural sector and for society at large.

1.24 GILL, G. J. **Farm Power in Bangladesh. Volume 1, A Comparative Analysis of Animal and Mechanical Farm Power in Bangladesh.** Development Study No. 9 (September 1981), Department of Agricultural Economics and Management, University of Reading, ENGLAND.

Discusses hypothetical advantages and disadvantages of tractorisation, the agricultural production and employment situation in Bangladesh, land resources and draught requirements and on farm power sources. A comparison of tractor and animal draught is presented, derived from a survey of farmers and analysis of available data. Draught animals are widely thought to be more reliable than machines by farmers, more available and also more versatile. Analysis of data showed no clear cut advantage of tractors in timeliness of operation as although a tractor enables faster cultivation it must justify higher capital investment by cultivating a higher total area than bullocks, therefore the period over which the machine is kept operational is extended and overall timeliness does not improve. In no case was cropping intensity at plot level found to correlate to the method of cultivation, and statistical analysis of yields indicate that tractor cultivated plots did not produce significantly higher yields than animal cultivated plots. Direct and indirect labour displacement effects are analysed and cost comparisons also made. The final conclusion of the study is that taking into account the full costs to society of using tractors there must be doubts as to whether substantial expansion of mechanisation is desirable, on the contrary there is a strong case for the improvement of animal powered equipment and techniques.

1.25 GOE, M.R. **Current Status of Research on Animal Traction.** World Animal Review 45, Jan-March 1983, pp. 2-16.

Article focusing on the technical aspects involved in employing animals as a source of power. Data are presented for draught capacity, nutrient requirements, crossbreeding for draught, working of cows, castration and training, yokes and harness design and implement draught. Discussion of these aspects conclude that a) Animal nutrition and optimum rates of work are two areas in need of further investigation; b) The assumption that cattle must possess a hump to be utilised for work is open to conjecture and should not hinder crossbreeding; c) Use of cows for draught would not be recommended when food supplies consist mainly of low-quality grazing; d) Data gathering methods should be improved by making more comparison between research stations and traditional farms; e) Research conducted for one or more complete cropping seasons should reduce errors in estimates of performance; f) Species other than cattle, horses, asses and buffalo should be given more consideration; g) Further consideration of the engineering principles involved in harnessing power from animal to implement will allow for an improvement in yoke harness and implement design.

SEE ALSO: **Animal Traction: Guidelines for Utilisation**, MSc Thesis presented to Cornell University, 1981.

Covers principles of animal draught, draught capacity of animals, situation of animal draught in warm climates (horses, asses and mules, buffalo, oxen, cows, camels and elephants) other species utilised for draught (yak, reindeer, llama and alpacka, dog, elk and moose, sheep and goat), comparative draught performance and nutrient requirements of draught animals. Concludes that few guidelines exist for individuals in agricultural programmes wishing to upgrade this area of livestock utility and that there is frequently a lack of interaction among government agencies responsible for agricultural development. There is considerable scope for improvement of harnessing systems. Identifies a dilemma on how best to match feed resources and animal needs, since it is difficult for animals in warm climate regions to obtain sufficient levels of TDN while grazing on natural pasture alone (except during the early part of the wet season) indicating a need for supplementary feed, which may be unavailable or too high in cost.

1.26 HARVEY, J. A. **The Costs of Providing Animal Draught - A Preliminary Investigation.** O.D.A. Technical Bulletin No. 1 (1973) Botswana.

Reviews fixed and variable costs of maintaining animals.

1.27 HASWELL, M. **Economic Choice of Appropriate Technology by Peasant Farmers.** in Report of the Rural Technology Meet for East, Central and Southern Africa, Yundum, The Gambia, and Dakar, Senegal, 14 - 22 May 1979, Commonwealth Secretariat.

Study on peasant family level (very general). Links labour input to crop output. Output is increased by oxen or tractors but the cost is also increased. Outlines conflict between farmers and economists values and advocates new technolgies which are available in quantity, easy to use and low cost.

1.28 HEDMAN, L. **The Horse is Back in Forestry** Swedish University of Agricultural Sciences, College of Forestry, Department of Operational Efficiency, S-770 73, Garpenberg, Sweden.

1.29 HUMPHRIES, C.P.; PEARSON, S.R. **Choice of Technique in Sahelian Rice Production.** Food Research Institute Studies, lXVll (3) (1979).

Profitability of various ways of growing rice. Found that the least cost combination of inputs in a technique occurred in the traditional swamp method and that the most effective method under a secure water control was irrigation with small pumps. Best methods were those using improved tools and animal traction (decreased costs by 10%).

1.30 INNS, F.M. **Animal Power in Agricultural Production Systems: With Special Reference to Tanzania.** World Animal Review 34; 2-10 (1980)

Discusses the case for animals vs. tractors giving cost calculations for a 50 Kw tractor and a pair of oxen. Concludes that economically the balance of advantage lies with the oxen, especially where foreign exchange is not easily available, farm size is modest and labour supply not a limiting factor. Looks also at characteristics of draught animal species and at farming systems and ox drawn implements in Tanzania. Concludes that existing animal powered systems in use in Tanzania could be improved especially from the point of view of soil moisture and conservation needs. The identification of a viable system is a prerequisiste to the identification of suitable equipment. The greater use of animals for general village transport as well as for farm use needs to be investigated.

1.31 JABBAR, M.A. **Need for Mechanising Tillage Operations in Bangladesh.** Paper presented at Symposium for the Mechanisation of Small Scale Peasant Farming, Hokkaido, JAPAN, 7-10 July 1980. (Department of Agricultural Economics, Bangladesh Agricultural University, Mymensingh, Bangladesh.)

Looks at current state of mechanisation of tillage (animal power with traditional implements). Finds substantial degradation in level of mechanisation due to absolute and increasing shortage of draught power evidenced by an increasing proportion of cows used for draught work (causing a decline in milk production and in animal reproduction), and degrading health condition of animals. The power problem is marked among small farms, larger landowners are better equipped but still inadequate power in relation to land owned. The neglect of the livestock sector led to some substitution of animals by tillers and tractors but agrarian structure and government policy favouring large owners constrain efficient use of new technology resulting in decreased production, increased polarisation and increased unemployment. Concludes that imported tillers and tractors have proved inappropriate under the present agrarian structure and recommends immediate attention to improving the efficiency of animal draught systems to solve the power shortage problem.

1.32 JOHNSON, B.F. **Farming Equipment Innovations and Rural Industrialisation In Eastern Africa; An Overview.** World Employment Programme Research, Working Paper No. 80 (Technology and Employment Programme) July 1980, I.L.O., Geneva.

Provides socioeconomic justification for the development and use of animal powered mechanical innovations compared to engine powered ones. Analyses how national economic policies (Kenya, Tanzania and Uganda) have diversely affected the rise in farm incomes which restrains the effective demand for farm equipment innovations. A lack of effective methodologies for research and development activities to generate and diffuse mechanical and tillage innovations is also discussed. Advocates a learning approach based on local constraints.

1.33 JOHNSON, B.F. **Socioeconomic Aspects of Improved Animal Drawn Implements and Mechanisation in Semi Arid East Africa.** In Proceedings, International Workshop on Socioeconomic Constraints to Development of Semi Arid Tropical Agriculture, Hyderabad, India, 19-23 February 1979. International Crops Research Institute for the Semi Arid Tropics. (I.C.R.I.S.A.T.) INDIA.

Principle hypothesis, research into animal power should be given high priority. Paper examines the socioeconomic factors most relevant to decisions concerning the role of animal drawn implements in the semi arid regions of Kenya, Tanzania and Uganda. Structural demographic features should be taken into consideration in determining national policies for agriculture, and industrial development also needs to be considered in determining agricultural research priorities and development strategies for these semi arid areas. These relationships are especially evident in Kenya where rural migration has been mainly responsible for the extremely rapid growth of population in the major farming areas. Attention is given to the present situation and future prospects in Kenya partly because they epitomise the fact that the technical problems of devising more productive and sustainable farming systems must be considered in relation to the broader problems of economic transformation and social modernisation.

1.34 KER, A.D.R. **The Development of Improved Farming Systems Based on Ox Cultivation.** Chapter 15, "Agricultural Policy Issues in East Africa", ed. V.F. Amann, Makerere University, Kampala, UGANDA, May 1973 (Faculty of Education, Makerere University).

Describes trials in growing cotton, groundnuts and finger millet on a management farm in Uganda. Ox based and tractor based systems are described and compared, with emphasis on operation times and costs of cultivation methods. The cost of growing all the crops using ox cultivation systems were lower than those using the tractor based systems. Concludes with policy recommmendations based on trial results.

1.35 KINSEY, B.H. **Agricultural Equipment Innovations and Rural Transformation in Tanzania** in "Farm Equipment Innovations in Eastern Africa" eds. Ahmed and Kinsey (1981) (a).

Discusses Tanzanian government policy on farm equipment
(stated and executed), patterns of use of equipment,
economic impact, constraints to ox cultivation, sources of
supply for farm implements, research and development
activities in screening and generating farm equipment
innovations. Indicates an inconsistency between declared
policy goals and programmes implemented and suggests that
tractors will remain uneconomic even with an increasing
village scale cultivation, but that a mix of manual, animal
and tractor based technologies may be appropriate.

1.36 KINSEY, B.H. **Equipment Innovations in Cotton-Millet Farming Systems in Uganda.** in "Farm Equipment Innovations in Eastern Africa" eds Aman and Kinsey (1981) (b).

Looks at existing cotton-millet farming systems in Uganda.
Rapid adoption of draught ox power failed to lead to a
process of cumulative change in which new items of equipment
were adopted in a gradual sequence as new bottlenecks were
encountered. Analysis indicates considerable potential for
increased output with use of oxen and a basic set of
equipment to overcome bottlenecks. Evidence of limited
adoption of ox drawn implements from past years research and
development equipment testing, argues that this is largely
due to lack of systems approach to equipment development,
inadequate technical testing without farm based trials or
analysis of likely costs and benefits and risk factors.
Also extension staff lacked technical expertise and
experience.

1.37 KINSEY, B.H. **Farm Equipment Innovations, Agricultural Growth and Employment in Zambia.** World Employment Research Working Paper No. 64 (Technology and Employment Programme), August 1980, I.L.O., Geneva.

First of a set (see above) of case studies on critical
reviews of farm equipment innovations in East, Central and
Southern Africa. Survey of existing and available
equipment, manual, oxdrawn and mechanical to find
appropriate small farm technology for maize cultivation.
Study reveals that oxdrawn planters have the greatest
potential for small and medium scale farmers. Presents a
list of criteria of technological appropriateness and
concludes with a discussion of broader policy dimensions in
Zambia.

1.38 KUNDU, P.B. **Draught Animal Power, its Use and Better Utilisation as the Source of Additional Energy.** National Seminar on DAP Systems in India, Bangalore, 1982.

1.39 LELE, U. **Tractors and Ox Ploughs in Africa** in "The Design of Rural Development; Lessons from Africa", Baltimore Md; The John Hopkins University Press (1975).

The pros and cons of introducing tractors and associated equipment as against equipment powered by oxen are examined in the light of African experiences in rural development projects. Concludes that both tractorisation and ox plough cultivation have a potential to increase productivity of small-holder agriculture, provided the associated inputs and innovations are introduced simultaneously. However, in most conditions ox cultivation may be preferable because of its relatively greater flexibility, lower cost and greater growth linkages with the rest of the economy.

1.40 LOCKERETZ, F.C. (ed) **Agriculture and Energy.** Academic Press, New York 1976.

1.41 MASUD, S.M.; UNDERWOOD, F.L. **Power in East Pakistan Farming: A Study of Work Animal Costs.** Farm Management Research Report No. 2, Mymensingh Bureau of Agricultural, Economic. Statistical, and Sociological Research, (1969) Faculty of Agricultural Economics and Rural Sociology, Pakistan Agricultural University.

Study of work animal costs in Pakistan. Shows cost of animal power to be a highly variable factor and makes recommendations for research into increasing the efficiency of animal power usage.

1.42 MIAN, M.S.J.; HUSSAIN, M.K. **A Comparative Study of the Economics of Cultivation by Bullock and Power Tiller in the Production of Transplanted Aman Paddy Rice in Some Selected Areas of Bangladesh.** PE and FM Research Report No. 1, October 1975, Mymensingh, INDIA.

1.43 MUCHIRI, G.; MINTO, S.D. **An Approach to Research and Development in Agricultural Mechanisation in Developing Countries,** in Report of the Rural Technology Meet for East, Central and Southern Africa, Arusha, TANZANIA, 1977. Commonwealth Secretariat.

Argues for multidisciplinary approach to research on agricultural mechanisation involvng sociologists, economists, agronomists and engineers. Proposes three level approach to research and development; a) Farmers acceptance trials b) Testing technology package under controlled conditions c) Undertaking fundamental research on particular factors such as crop varieties or soil moisture regime. Research and development at these three levels should be conducted concurrently.

1.44 MUNZINGER, P. **Economic Aspects of Using Draught Animals.** Part B/1V in "Animal Traction in Africa" compiled by P. Munzinger, G.T.Z. 1982.

Divided into discussions of microecomonic and macroeconomic effects of using animal traction. Includes presentation of empirical findings regarding profitability in comparison with other levels of mechanisation. Aims to present an instrument which makes it possible to determine rather than simply discuss the advantages and disadvantages of animal traction and evaluate them accordingly. Concludes that animal traction is more economic in the long term where relatively cheap labour and sufficient land are available simultaneously; animal traction is primarily suitable for smallholdings; the use of draught animals is relatively independent of the labour structure on the farm but tends to reduce the need for outside labour; easy access to credit is required to adopt animal traction for most farmers; in some parts of Africa local prices compared with tractors suggests that animals should be used more, especially where few suitable energy raw materials exist; an important microeconomic advantage is to provide opportunities to earn additional non-agricultural income. A general discussion follows of potential macroeconomic effects of the use of draught animals from the point of view of the contribution they can make to achieving national economic targets and the nature of the macroeconomic expenditure they cause.

1.45 OLOUFA, M.M. **Sell That Tractor While Still Running** Paper presented at Expert Consultation on Appropriate Use of Animal Energy in Agriculture in Africa and Asia, F.A.O., Rome, ITALY, November 15-19 1982.

Discussion of advantage of using animal power in Tanzania rather than tractors with the shortages and high costs of spare parts and fuel. Covers choice and care of animals with comparisons of time and cost of cultivation by hand, with draught animals and with power equipment.

1.46 POLLARD, S.J.; WAINAINA, C.K. **Oxen or Tractors.**
Part 1, Livestock International 10 (3); 62-63 June/July 1982
Part 2, "   "   10 (4); 94-95 August/ September 1982
Part 3, Livestock International 10 (5); 121-122 October/ November 1982

The basis of these articles were three studies of smallholder demand for mechanisation undertaken by the Agricultural Economics section of the Kenyan Ministry of Agriculture's machinery testing unit on Nakarau. The study covered three systems of farming, tractor cultivation, ox cultivation and 'jembe' (hand cultivation). Discusses Kenyan smallholder agriculture and examines the factors which influence the farmers choice of technology; cropping, farming and household objectives; the existing and potential farm bottlenecks; the comparative process and costs of using and owning and the opportunity cost of alternative power sources and tools; the comparative availablility, reliability and returns, versatility and convenience; the farmers present and projected net income. Concludes that tractors are more expensive, less available, less reliable and versatile but more convenient than oxen, therefore farmers prefer tractors. But in the interests of the national economy oxen should be promoted above tractors to enable lower costs of cultivation, more timely cultivation, greater food production and savings in foreign exchange.

1.47 REDDY, C.V. **Role of Draught Animals as Alternate Energy Source in Agriculture.** National Seminar on DAP Systems in India, Bangalore 1982.

1.48 RYAN, M.; ABEYRATNE, F.; FARRINGTON, J. **Animal Draught – The Economics of Revival.** Occasional Publication No. 23, June 1981, Agrarian Research and Training Institute, P.O. Box 1522, Colombo 7, SRI LANKA.

Paper draws on farm management data collected from farmers at three major colonisation schemes in Sri Lanka between August 1970 and October 1980. A comparison of tractor and buffalo operating costs provides strong economic justification for expanding the role of animal power in cultivation. Imperfections in the farm power hire market prevent such real discrepancies in operating costs from being translated into hire charge differences at the farm gate which in turn leaves the demand for tractor custom services high. The thrust of the paper is that this imbalance cannot be rectified by intervention in the farm power hire market but proposes that what is needed is a concerted effort to broaden the base of ownership of power, expecially draught animals. Discusses a range of issues relevant to a policy of ownership, the poor quality of current statistical information on the national herd, the patterns of distribution and use of animal draught and a consideration of the options of animal husbandry systems with an overview of the profitability of each system.

1.49 SHARMA, R.K. **Economics of Tractor Vs. Bullock Cultivation.** Agricultural Economics Research Centre, University of Delhi, India, 1972.

1.50 SINGH, I. **A Note on the Economics of Agricultural Mechanisation.** Studies in Employment and Rural Development No. 33, 1976, Development Economics Department, International Bank for Reconstruction and Development. (World Bank).

An analysis of the economic implications of alternative forms of mechanisation in Sukumaland, Tanzania (ox and tractor based), taking into consideration important factors of a) Seasonality and farm level resource endowment b) The nature of fixed costs and economies of scale c) The real opportunity costs of inputs, especially farm labour d) The output mix e) Government policies relating to input and output prices and distribution of inputs. Emphases need to go beyond partial budgeting approaches to the use of linear programming farm and village level models.

1.51 SINGH, I.; SUBRAMANIUM, J. **Appropriate Technologies in Tanzanian Agriculture: Some Empirical and Policy Considerations.** Annex V11 of World Bank Official Report 1977, "Tanzania - Basic Economic Report".

Sets criteria for appropriate technology in peasant society. Presents empirical evidence from a number of studies on agricultural technologies in Tanzania to see how they meet the operational criteria established. Specifically concludes that irrespective of the intensity of tractor use or the opportunity costs of labour, oxen dominate in terms of economic efficiency in Sukumaland. Oxen cultivation is also socially more acceptable. Generally concludes that no one solution should be accepted for any country as diverse as Tanzania; locally identified conditions should determine the choice of technology; the economically efficient technology is also often the most appropriate. Recommends increased attention to the development of a greater variety of locally produced tools, greater emphasis on the softwares of the technology (education, extension, support systems) and decentralisation of decisions relating to agricultural technologies.

1.52 SLEEPER, J.A. **An Economic Analysis of the Role of Ox Ploughing and Cattle Feeding in the Stratification of West African Livestock Production.** Masters Dissertation, Michigan State University, East Lansing, Michigan, U.S.A.

1.53 STARKEY, P; VERHAEGHE, H. **Weed Control in Maize Using Draught Animals.** Livestock International 10 (3); 64-69 June/July 1982.

Report on comparative trials on the growth of maize to investigate the use of multipurpose animal powered toolbars and compare their effectiveness in weed control with the use of hand labour and tractor cultivation. Results show that weed regrowth is significantly less following ploughing with oxen or tractors than following hand cultivation. Weed regrowth is also significantly reduced following weeding with ox drawn tines than following hand weeding. Concludes that ox cultivation is not only technically preferable but also economically beneficial, resulting in the highest gross margin for maize cultivation.

1.54 STOCKING, M. **Tractors, Oxen, or a Mixture of Both?** International Agricultural Development 1 (8); 10:11 September 1981.

Discusses results of an analysis by AGRIPLAN (an F.A.O. funded scheme to promote local design and implementation of projects) of the relative merits and drawbacks of hoe, oxen and tractor cultivation in Zambia. The results show that maize yields from tractor farmers are the lowest and profits from the oxen owners the highest. Concludes that the promotion of ox ownership and cultivation could provide the key to long term security for farmers and the national feed supply.

1.55 STOKES, A.R. **Mechanisation and the Peasant Farmer.** World Crops 15:444-450 December 1963.

A report on the impact of the tractor on upland farming in Northern Nigeria. Concludes that improved ox drawn machinery, which can be used to take advantage of the greater yield potential of tie ridge farming, offers the greatest hope of increasing the productivity of small farms, a problem on which the tractor has made little or no impact. Ox drawn implements are compared and production costs tabulated for each implement.

1.56 STRACHAN, G. **Sources of Draught Power in U.K. Farming Systems.** Undergraduate Dissertation, 1983, School of Development Studies, University of East Anglia, Norwich, ENGLAND.

Hypothesis, due to rising oil prices in the 1970's the horse may have a role to play on small mixed farms in the U.K. Gives historic perspective to the three sources of draught power that have been used in the U.K., a discussion of the energy efficiency of modern agriculture and the need for a future low energy input farming system. Reviews research into draught animal systems and present methods for calculating the nutritional requirements of the animals. Description and results of trials, carried out at the Rural Technology Unit at the School of Development Studies, designed to compare the efficiency of ox, horse and tractor draught.

1.57 SUBRAMANYUM, K.V.; RYAN, J.G. **Livestock as a Source of Power in Indian Agriculture.** Occasional Paper No. 12, International Crops Research Institute for the Semi Arid Tropics. (I.C.R.I.S.A.T.) (1975)

Looks at livestock distribution, breed, size, days of employment/month. Economic aspects of bullock power. Recommends bullocks should be used at least 200 days/year. Analyses costs of bullocks and tractors.

1.58 THIERSTEIN, G.F. **Crop Yields and Net Profit for Man, Animal and Mechanical Power in East Africa.** A.S.A.E Annual Meeting, Paper 75-515, Logan, Utah, U.S.A.

1.59 WARD, G.M.; SUTHERLAND, T.M.; SUTHERLAND, J.M. **Animals as an Energy Source in Third World Agriculture.** Science Vol. 208, 1980.

4.2 Situational Analysis - Impact, Adoption and Diffusion

2.1 ANDERSON, F.M. **Draught Animal Power in Africa - An Overview.** Working Paper No. 3, Expert Consultation on Appropriate Use of Animal Energy in Agriculture in Africa and Asia, 15-19 November 1982, F.A.O., Rome, Italy. (I.L.C.A., Addis Ababa, Ethiopia).

General discussion of the characteristics of the existing situation with draught animals in Africa, constraints to the development of DAP and future prospects.

2.2 BAKER, P.R. **An Evaluation of Past Developments in the Field of Ox Cultivation in Central Province.** AGRIPLAN 1981, (F.A.O. Report), Box 1250, Kabwe, Zambia. (Overseas Development Group, School of Development Studies, University of East Anglia, Norwich, England).

Reviews policy regarding ox power in Zambia from colonial times. Discusses constraints to the development of ox cultivation (locational and institutional), and results of development policy. Reviews projects for the development of ox power ansd the lessons to be learnt from these, and concludes that the total effort directed at ox farmers remains negligible. Recommends establishment of a co-ordinated programme aiming to strengthen support for the ox farmer.

2.3 BARRETT, V.; LASSITER, G.; BAKER,D.; CRAWFORD, E. **Animal Traction in Eastern Upper Volta - A Technical, Economic and Institutional Analysis.** MSU International Development Paper No. 4, 1982, Department of Agricultural Economics, Michegan State University, East Lansing, Michegan, 48824, U.S.A.

Describes 1975-1981 animal traction programme. Reviews historical context and evaluates the institutional performance of the programme. Problems occurring include lack of reliable marketing outlets and lack of improved biological and mechanical technologies. Nevertheless, project has improved on previous efforts in stressing a broader approach to farmer adoption and avoiding the limited 'model farm' approach; incorporating improved equipment manufacture and repair systems; utilising donkey traction as well as oxen and allowing farmers to choose their own cropping pattern, thus adapting to regional agroclimatic and resource conditions. Finds that overall provision of vital support services (extension and training, marketing, credit, equipment services and livestock and veterinary services) has been inadequate and has impeded the success of animal traction use. Six areas of technical impact are covered; a) Equipment utilisation, b) Other use of animals, c) Acreage effects, d) Cropping mix effects, e) Yield effects, f) Effects on household labour allocation. The economic analysis compares animal traction farmers and hoe farmers in terms of cropping income, farm and household income and annual and monthly cash flows. Overall survey data indicates that the technical and economic performance of animal traction at farm level has not been dramatically different from hoe farming, due to the recent adoption of animal traction, poor programme performance and lack of experience of most farmers. Concludes with discussion of specific measures which can be undertaken to overcome problems of programme.

2.4 CARSON, S.P. **Project of the Government of Mozambique - Proposed Animal Traction Project.** F.A.O./U.N.D.P., Rome, Italy.

2.5 CLARKE, N.A. **The Contribution of Draught Animals to the Livestock Sector in Sind.** F.A.O./U.N.D.P. Project PAK/74/018 1979.

2.6 CREASY, J.S. **The Draught Ox.** Heavy Horse Magazine March 1977, pp 26-29.

Account of draught oxen used in agriculture in Britain from ancient times to the early nineteenth century, comparing the efficiency of oxen and horses.

2.7 DELGADO, C.L.; McINTIRE, J. **Constraints on Oxen Cultivation in the Sahel.** American Journal of Agricultural Economics 64 (2) : 188-196 (1982).

Ox powered cultivation is common in parts of the Sahel yet most farmers in the region continue to cultivate manually. Insights from ox farms in Mali are compared to non-adopters in Upper Volta. Ox power technology may be more labour shifting than labour saving, linear programming models indicate a prohibitive opportunity cost of extra labour required for team maintenance and use on small rainfed farms growing traditional millets and sorghum in Upper Volta. Farm simulations suggest the ox ploughing increases cash crop acreage but clearly profitable adoption requires companion innovaions to boost labour productivity at peak periods.

2.8 EICHER, C.K. AND BAKER, D.C. **Research on Agricultural Development in Sub-Saharan Africa : A Critical Survey.** Michigan State University International Development Paper No. 1, 1982.

Part V **Technical Change.** Animal and tractor mechanisation.

Reviews history of animal and tractor mechanisation schemes in Africa and the crucial policy question of what types of mechanical power are appropriate. Discusses methodological problems in carrying out research on mechanisation and points to inadequacy of basic data on yield and acreage effects of animal traction at farm level. Reviews ex-post studies of animal traction schemes, concluding that there is a range if technical, economic and logistic constraints on the spread of total packages of animal traction in Africa, and consequently complete animal traction packages cannot serve as an engine of growth of agriculture in Africa. Selective mechanisation - farmers replacing one implement at a time - should be facilitated and major attention should be directed to improved agronomic practices which can complement animal traction. Tractor mechanisation also is plagued with technical, economic and instructional problems, although it will become increasingly financially profitable for farmers and government to carry out farming tasks, such as land preparation, with tractors as rural wage rates rise. General conclusion however, is that hand and animal power will undoubtedly remain the major power source in Africa in the 1980s and should receive the bulk of research support.

2.9 FARM MACHINERY RESEARCH UNIT (ZAMBIA). **Manufacture and Introduction of Hand and Animal Drawn Implements.** Project No. 4, Regional Appropriate Technology Programme, F.M.R.U., Department of Agriculture, Magoye, ZAMBIA.

Report on Zambia's experience in the manufacture and marketing of hand operated and animal drawn equipment. Sets out the prevailing situation and attempts to explain the difficulties and constraints involved, summarised as lack of knowledge in manufacture, difficultues in arranging local credit and foreign exchange, overall shortage of imported raw materials, lack of effective competition in the sale of equipment and difficulties in mounting and sustaining programmes of extension and training in the increased use of traditional and improved animal drawn equipment.

2.10 FERNSEBNER, R. **Development of Draught Animal Use in the N.W. Province of Zambia.** Report to G.T.Z., 1979, Eschborn, GERMANY.

2.11 FOOD AND AGRICULTURE ORGANISATION OF THE UNITED NATIONS. **Assistance in Agricultural Mechanisation.** F.A.O. Mission Report, 1974, Rome, Italy.

Review of present situation, a) Activities of government rural agencies, b) Mechanisation and rural development; oxen, tractors, field support and planning, c) Education, research and development. Gives details of a research programme for the promotion, extension and better utilisation of ox drawn equipment.

2.12 F.A.O. **Guidelines for a Technical Survey on Draught Animal Power.** F.A.O., Rome, Italy, 1980.

Outine of a survey originated by N.S. Ramaswamy for the F.A.O. to discover a) Geographical distribution of draught animals, b) Numbers, breeds and working life of animals, c) Value and health, d) Operations, e) Institutions for draught animal power development.

2.13 F.A.O. **Perspective Study of Agricultural Development for Zambia: Farm Mechanisation** F.A.O. Rome, Italy, 1976.

Taking into account the various sizes of farms and the socioeconomic position the document attempts to determine demand for animal draught and tractors and the likely supply and costings.

2.14 FENG YANG LIAN. **The Use of Draught Cattle in China.** Working Paper No. 6, Expert Consultation on Appropriate Use of Animal Energy in Agriculture in Africa and Asia, 15-19 November 1982, F.A.O., Rome, Italy. (Department of Animal Science, Beijing Agricultural University, Beijing, China).

General discussion of draught cattle in agriculture in China with data on draught power and working capacity of yellow cattle, energy requirements and other species utilised (buffaloes, yaks).

2.15 FULTON, D. AND TOULMIN, D. **A Socioeconomic Study of an Agropastoral System in Central Mali.** Unpublished Report for I.L.C.A., 1982.

Data are presented on the capital and maintenance costs of ox plough teams and donkey plough teams, these costs are then spread over different farm sizes to assess per hectare costs of each form of traction. The actual distribution of animal traction equipment in two villages is discussed and ways in which a household owning no equipment can get acess to a plough team. Data are then presented to show the uses of animal traction in the system and its importance to different crops and operations. The effects of the introduction of animal traction are discussed in relation to the farming system of the area. The effects relate to; a) Field size, b) The fallowing system, c) Yields per hectare, d) Plant densities, e) Crop composition, f) Labour productivitiy, g) Household unity.

2.16 GILL, G.J. **Farm Power in Bangladesh - Volume 1, A Comparative Analysis of Animal and Mechanical Power in Bangladesh**

SEE ENTRY 1.24

2.17 GOVERNMENT OF BANGLADESH. **Livestock and Draught Power Development.** F.A.O./U.N.D.P. Mission, Working Report V, August 1978.

2.18 GOVERNMENT OF INDIA. **Socioeconomic Study of Animal Drawn Transport in the Rural Areas of the Country. Summary of Findings.** Ministry of Shipping and Transport, 1980.

2.19 GREGOIRE, R. **(Animal Traction and Stock Raising in the Sudan Sahel Zone).** Courier, 37: 31-34 1976.

2.20 HAUG, H. AND GERNER-HAUG, I. **Promotion of Draught Animal Traction Through the Supply of Simple Agricultural Equipment.** Part C/11 in 'Animal Traction in Africa' compiled by P. Munzinger, G.T.Z., 1982.

Outlines the paramount targets for agricultural policy in Mali and details the projects seen as a major means of implementing the recommended strategy - Agricultural training and promotion of draught animals as an appropriate form of agricultural mechanisation. Discusses problems and major obstacles to the project, such as, difficulties in procurement and distribution of animals and equipment and organisation of credit repayments. Concludes that on the basis of the positive experience gained to date it can be expected that draught animals will continue to maintain their position in Mali's agriculture, especially since economic conditions for tractorisation are continually deteriorating and the necessary infrastructure will not be available in the forseeable future.

2.21 HEYER, J. **A Preliminary Report on Farm Surveys: Tractor and Ox Cultivation in Makueni and Bungoma.** In Proceedings of a workshop on Farm Equipment Innovations for Agricultural Development and Rural Industrialisation. Occasional Paper No. 16, 1975, Institute of Development Studies, University of Nairobi, KENYA.

Presents preliminary findings of a 1974 survey of the use of tractors and oxen. Looks at reasons for tractor and oxen adoption and non-adoption in two areas of different rainfall and presents an analysis of potential effects of increased costs.

2.22 INTERNATIONAL LIVESTOCK CENTRE FOR AFRICA. (I.L.C.A.) **Animal Traction in SubSaharan Africa.** I.L.C.A. Bulletin No. 14, December 1981.

Covers a) Contribution of animal traction to Africa, estimating present and prospective contribution in terms of number of hectares/year covered and power provided by animals as a proportion of total power contribution. b) Farmers application of animal traction and bioclimatic, traditional and historical factors influencing the way AT is used. c) The constraints to efficient use of AT; tsetse fly, nature and availability of cattle, cultivation implements and harnesses, feed resources, social constraints, management and financial constraints. d) The lessons of development experience, adoption of AT, impact on farm productivity and income and macroeconomic impact. Concludes that despite inadequate information and monitoring AT is increasing in a number of areas and indicates that the practice could bring substantial benefits to crop and livestock production.

2.23 INNS, F.M. **Animal Power in Agricultural Production Systems; With Special Reference to Tanzania.**

SEE ENTRY 1.30

2.24 KALB, D. **Sociological Aspects of the Use of Draught Animals on African Smallholdings.** Part B/V in 'Animal Traction in Africa', compiled by P. Munzinger, G.T.Z. 1982.

Survey of the most important sociological factors involved in promotion of animal traction in African smallholdings within the limitations of inadequate empirical data on this aspect. Looks first at social characteristics of African smallholders, covering division of labour and cultural identity, social stratification, land law, features of production strategies and taboos. Continues to look at sociological aspects of implementation of AT projects, giving general criteria covering processes of innovation and adoption.

2.25 KJAERBY, F. **Problems and Contradictions in the Development of Ox Cultivation in Tanzania.** Research Report No. 66, Centre for Development Research, Copenhagen, and Scandinavian Institute of African Studies, Uppsala, 1983. (Centre for Development Research, Ny Kongensgade 9 DK-1472, Copenhagen, Denmark).

Traces the historical development of ox cultivation in Tanzania, the social economic and political causes which have determined its spread, the uneven spatial expansion and limited individual adoption. Describes the evolution of land use systems (indicating the systems in which ox cultivation is found) and discusses the question of labour productivity. Focuses more specifically on agropastoralism, the most common system of land use in which ox ploughing has expanded. Also contains an analysis of the socioeconomic effects of ox cultivation in comparison to hoe cultivation; a critical review of agricultural mechanisation policy of the government during the 1960's and 1970's; and evaluation of ox implements found in Tanzania, with recommendations for further research into more appropriate implements. Concludes with discussion of development perspectives of some of the crucial problems related to the further development of comprehensive ox mechanisation, (land use in the context of villageisation and unequal access to productive forces and labour power). Makes recommendations for priorities in research.

2.26 KINSEY, B.H. **Agricultural Equipment Innovations and Rural Transformation in Tanzania.**

SEE ENTRY 1.35

2.27 KINSEY, B.H. **Equipment Innovations in Cotton Millet Farming Systems in Uganda.**

SEE ENTRY 1.36

2.28 KINSEY, B.H. **Farm Equipment Innovations, Agricultural Growth and Employment in Zambia.**

SEE ENTRY 1.37

2.29 LASSITER, G. **The Impact of Animal Traction on Farming Systems in E. Upper Volta.** Ph.D Dissertation, 1982, Cornell University, Ithaca, New Yark.

2.30 LAURENT, C.K. **The Use of Bullocks for Power on Farms in Northern Nigeria.** Bulletin of Rural Economics and Sociology 3 (2), Department of Agricultural Economics, University of Ibadan, Nigeria.

Massive adoption of bullocks by farmers, therefore massive market for farm implements. Argues that adoption is a result of the control of tsetse fly. Implements and farmers skills must improve.

2.31 LE MOIGNE, M. **Animal Draught Cultivation in Francophone Africa.** In Proceedings, International Workshop on Socioeconomic Constraints to the Development of Semi Arid Tropical Agriculture, Hyderabad, India 19-23 February 1979. I.C.R.I.S.A.T., INDIA.

History of animal draught cultivation in West Africa. Lists equipment in use with details of equipment numbers, density and present research. Briefly discusses factors determining the spread of AD cultivation and concludes that scope for animal draught remains limited, therefore must also consider other technical solutions, herbicides and power machinery for harvesting and threshing.

2.32 LINK, H.; KALB, D. **Support of Agricultural Mechanisation - Especially Oxenisation - in Tanga Region, Tanzania.** Report to G.T.Z., 1980, Eschborn, Germany.

2.33 METTRICK, H. **Oxenisation in the Gambia - An Evaluation.** Ministry of Overseas Development Report EV 14. (1978) (University of Reading, U.K.).

Discussion of the development of appropriate implements in the Gambia (the failure of the Aplos toolframe and success of the Sine Hoe package), possibilities for the use of horses and donkeys, and policy issues (credit, role of farm centres, local production of implements). Evaluates; a) The impact of oxenisation on production - largely confined to the groundnut crop, and concludes that limited impact arises from mechanisation of only one operation, primary cultivation. b) The spread of oxenisation, points to lack of data and increasing preference for horses and donkeys. c) Costs and benefits, suggests an improvement to family income of 10-20%. d) Social aspects, wealth, status and role of women. e) The role of aid. Concludes with discussion of factors favouring adoption, a) The availability of a simple and appropriate technology, b) Social structure, c) Proximity for Senegal (with a concurrent development of appropriate technology, presence of manufacturers and availability of well tried implements, well tried credit system available), d) Marketing is efficient, with stable price regime for groundnuts.

2.34 METTRICK, H.M.; JAMES, D.P. **Farm Power in Bangladesh - Volume 2. Part 1; Some Aspects of the Economics of Farm Power; Part 2; Mechanisation and Institutions on Noakhali.** Development Study No. 20, September 1981, Department of Agricultural Economics and Management, University of Reading, England.

Part 1. (Mettrick) Analysis of several aspects of draught power in Bangladesh. Covers a) The availability of draught power, results indicating that there is likely to be a continual deterioration in supply. b) Demand for draught power, focussing on two different concepts of the indivisibility of draught power. The availability of animals at peak periods appears to be the limiting factor. Results of the survey indicate that the maximum number of farmers with access to adequate draught power is approximately 30% in some areas and considerably less in others. c) The use of cows for draught, a contributory factor to the low productivity of the herds. d) The cost of animal draught, using a model developed for Pakistan to calculate the structure and requirements of the herd necessary to support one draught animal. (SEE ENTRY 4.1.9) It appears that the cost of each ox equivalent is less in herds with draught females than in those without. e) Sharecropping and draught power. Overall results indicate a precarious situation with deteriorating availability of draught power likely for the next few years at least. Concludes with research and policy recommendations, especially in the area of nutrition and herd productivity.
Part 2. (James) Results of a socioeconomic analysis of resources, social structure and institutions on Noakhali, Bangladesh, and a discussion of the implications which the introduction of tractors may have for field cultivation and socioeconomic change.

2.35 MINISTRY OF FINANCE AND ECONOMIC PLANNING - SUDAN **Jebel Marra Rural Development Project Annual Report 1981-82.** Annexe 1, Agricultural Services Department, August 1982.

Details research undertaken by five divisions - Extension, Adaptive Research, Horticulture, Forestry, Credit and Marketing. Project 2 - cultivation systems - within the adaptive research division details a survey into the impact of the use of animal drawn ploughs with regard to yield, cultivated area and distribution of benefits. Results indicate an approximate doubling in area cultivated for owners and renters; higher yields of millet and sorghum; farmers preference for camels; benefits larger for plough owners than for renters but the extent of hiring helps to spread benefits to a wider group of farmers. Discusses quality of locally made camel plough and concludes that there are technically no further alternatives. Recommendations are made for further research, monitoring and evaluation.

2.36 MOCZARSKI, S.Z. **Oxenisation in the Gambia; An Agricultural, Economic and Social Revolution.** The Gambia Ministry of Agriculture, 1966.

2.37 MUNZINGER, P. **Development and Situation of Animal Traction in Africa and Conditions Limiting Further Promotion.** Part A in 'Animal Traction in Africa', compiled by P., Munzinger, G.T.Z., 1982.

General assessment of animal traction in comparison with other forms of mechanisation. Draught animals are important as major problems limit the use of modern technology. (e.g. Capital, small holdings, lack of training, inadequate infrastructure). Gives detailed information on the use of draught animals historically and currently in Africa by region. Lists manufacturers of animal drawn equipment and national and international organisations with experience in promoting the use of draught animals. Discusses conditions restricting the use of and factors influencing draught animals under three headings; a) Natural environmental factors, b) Sociological and ethnological factors, c) Economic and institutional factors. Provides a detailed checklist for planning animal traction projects.

2.38 NEUNHAUSER, P. (ed) **Possibilities of the Introduction of Draught Animals in the North West Province of the United Republic of Cameroon.** Consultative study for G.T.Z. 1977.

Comprehensive study concerning the possibilities for the implementation of a draught animal programme in Cameroon. Presents; a) Judgement of the preconditions for implementation, environmental and socioeconomic, b) A critical analysis of the draught animal projects of the WUM area development agency outlining production technology, experience with crop production, economic analysis of possible farm organisations and proposals for a further WADA training programme, c) An analysis of four different approaches to the introduction of draught animals in West Africa (N. Nigeria, Mali, Ghana, Chad) with conclusions drawn for successful introduction, d) A report on the conditions and potential for the project implementation, with proposals.

2.39 ODEND'HAL, S. **Past, Present and Future Research on Livestock in Bangladesh - With Particular Emphasis on Draught Power and Mechanisation.** Report No. 49, The Ford Foundation, P.O. Box 49, Ramina, Dacca. 1978.

The current statistics, research and development aspects of the livestock of Bangladesh were examined by consultation with university, government and private officials and published documents. The results indicate a lack of reliable statistics, little research relevant to the village situation and a policy favouring academic evaluation of intensive livestock production not feasible in the country. Recommends the development of a livestock statistics unit in the livestock directorate.

2.40 OKAI, M. **The Development of Ox Cultivation in Uganda.** Eastern African Journal of Rural Development 8 (1-2); 191-215, 1975.

Study of ox cultivation practices in Uganda, covers a history of the promotion and expansion of ox cultivation and notes on ox training and equipment testing and development. Presents an analysis of field investigations that the agriculture of the area would rapidly improve if the economic capital, social and educational constraints holding back widespread adoption of ox cultivation were given such attention as that being given to the development of tractor cultivation.

2.41 OREV, Y. **Animal Draught in West Africa.** World Crops September/October 1972.

Outlines advantages and disadvantages of animal draught cultivation in Senegal and discusses how to begin the process of animal drawn agriculture in West Africa. Major problem is shortage of animal feeds, suggests answer is Guinea Bluestem. Concludes that since serious agronomic, social and aconomic obstacles exist better to concentrate on milk and meat production rather than power from animals.

2.42 RAO, A.R.; SING, I.J. **Bullocks, The Mainstay of Farm Power in India**, in 'Agriculture and Energy', (ed) W. Lockeretz, Academic Press, New York, 1976.

2.43 RICHARDS, J.I. **The Role of Draught Cattle in the Agricultural Development of Bangladesh.** Report to the Centre for Tropical Veterinary Medicine and Ministry of Overseas Development, C.T.V.M., University of Edinburgh, 1979.

Results of an investigation to estimate the current state of research work on animal draught in Bangladesh, assess the requirements for animal draught in relation to feed available, identify possible village case studies, explore possibilities of institutional links and assess scope for analysing village level data collected by the Reading University mechanisation project. Looks at; demographic history, land use, cropping systems, cattle statistics, power requirements, feed and fodder. Finds no depth research into animal draught by either government or aid organisations. Recommends programme on alternative feeds and improvement of existing feeds/crops for cattle at village level, consideration of the constraints to the development of animal production and a projct to improve the quality of service of animal husbandry extension officers.

2.44 ROLLINSON, D.H.L.; NELL, A.J. **The Present and Future Situation of Working Cattle and Buffalo in Indonesia.** U.N.D.P./F.A.O. Project INS/72/009 1973 Supporting Livestock Planning Working Paper, F.A.O., Rome, Italy.

2.45 RYAN, M.J.; ABEYRATNE, F.; FARRINGTON, J. **The Utilisation of Buffaloes for Farm Power in Sri Lanka.** Paper presented at Workshop on Water Buffalo Research in Sri Lanka, 24-28 November 1980, University of Peradeniya, Sri Lanka.

Reviews the role of buffaloes in small scale farming, comparing tractor and buffalo operating costs. Concludes strong economic justification for animal power. Attention drawn to the inadequacy of animal statistical information on buffalo population. Suggests that role of buffaloes could be expanded by wider use of ploughs instead of trampling and by transfer of adult and juvenile animals from areas of low to areas of high intensity. In longer term policies to promote stall feeding systems are essential.

2.46 SAMSON, B.T.; HERRARA, W.A.T.; HARWOOD, R.R. **Draught Animals in an Intensively Farmed Upland Rice Area in the Philippines.** International Rice Research Institute (I.R.R.I.) Saturday Seminar Paper, June 21st 1975.

Briefly discusses question of place of animals in agriculture. Outlines experiences relative to the use of draught animals gained while researching cropping systems in the province of Batangas. Covers characteristics, acquisition, work capacity and training of animals, local factors affecting work capacity and tillage capabilitiy and details of feeding. Concludes that draught animals furnish an efficient and economic source of power on small upland farms in intensive systems of cropping.

2.47 SARGENT, M.W. **A Village Level Extension Guide for the Introduction and Maintenance of Animal Traction.** Department of Agricultural Economics, Michigan State University, East Lansing, Michigan, U.S.A., 1979.

2.48 SARGENT, M.W. **Recommendations to National Government and International Donors for the Design and Implementation of Animal Traction Programmes.** Michigan State University, 1979.

2.49 SARGENT, M.W. **A Provincial Planning and Implementation Guide for the Introduction and Maintenance of Animal Traction.** Michigan State University 1979.

2.50 SARGENT, M.W.; LICHTE, J.A.; MATLON, P.J.; BLOOM, R. **An Assessment of Animal Traction in Francophone West Africa.** Working Paper No. 4, 1981, African Rural Economy Programme, Department of Agricultural Economics, Michigan State University, East Lansing, Michigan, U.S.A.

Report based on a review of 125 animal traction projects in West Africa, and on data obtained from 27 of the projects. Includes; a) Brief description of the characteristics of a model farming system based on the use of draught animal technology. b) A brief history of the introduction of DAP in the region. c) Summary of technical evidence of the effects of animal traction on productivity. The major technical, economic and institutional elements of the 27 projects are compared and key problems identified and evaluated.

2.51 SCHUTER, W.A.; VAN DER VEEN, M.G. **Economic Constraints on Agricultural Technology Adoption in Developing Nations.** Occasional Paper No. 5, 1977, Pennsylvania State University, U.S.A.I.D. Contract (no. AID/CM ta-147-442).

Economic review of agricultural technology, H.Y.Vs, oxen, tractors, pumps, etc. Constraints on technology adoption, farm size, tenancy, labour, capital, markets, prices, risk and uncertainty. Implications of this for programmes and research (e.g. must aim at utilisation, not adoption, see if technical operation is possible at farm level, increase knowledge of farm family conditions).

2.52 SMID, J. **Use of Draught Oxen in Northern Ghana.** Part C/IV in 'Animal Traction in Africa' compiled by P. Munzinger, G.T.Z. 1982.

Report on the promotion of draught animals in Ghana within the Ghana-German Agricultural Development Project. (G.G.A.D.P.). The background experience and results of the project are discussed.

2.53 STARKEY, P. (a) **Farming with Work Oxen in Sierra Leone.** (unpub)Information from; P. Starkey, Farm Director, Njala University College, Private Bag, Freetown, Sierra Leone.

Report on a work oxen project launched in 1979 in Sierra Leone. Covers the history of draught animal projects in Sierra Leone, the training and management of oxen, details of technique of farming with Ndama cattle, a review of different types of oxdrawn equipment tested, results of experimental trials undertaken, and a discussion of the economic costs and benefits of farming with work oxen. Concludes that the use of oxen for farm operations is a viable and attractive method of increasing both agricultural output and the efficiency of agricultural operations in Sierra Leone.

2.54 STARKEY, P. (b) **The Sierra Leone Work Oxen Project.** Appropriate Technology 8 (1): June 1981.

Reviews previous work oxen schemes in Sierra Leone and reports on the objectives, approach and prospects of the project launched in 1979.

2.55 TANGA INTEGRATED RURAL DEVELOPMENT PROGRAMME. **Pilot Project for Oxenisation at Mwanyumba Village.** TIRDEP, Tanga, Tanzania, October 1980.

Results of a sociological survey of attitudes and opinions of farmers and their willingness to cooperate, with the objective of checking the preconditions for a successful implementation of an oenisation project in a pilot village in the Tanga region. Report recommends a project approach based on communal ownership of oxen and implements and proposes a suitable organisational set-up.

2.56 TRAN VAN NHIEU, J. **Animal Traction in Madagascar.** Part C/111 in 'Animal Traction in Africa' compiled by P. Munzinger, G.T.Z. 1982.

Preconditions for the use of draught animals in Madagascar are extremely favourable, with a large number of cattle and local traditions favouring stockkeeping. Promotional organisation aims to improve the situation of the rural population by means of improved animal drawn implements, the setting up of local manufacture of implements, support of extension and veterinary services and the breeding and selection of more efficient draught animals. Details all aspects of animal traction situation in Madagascar; breeds, financing, feeding, equipment, distribution, types of farms, extension services, credit situation and some problems encountered in the use of draught animals. Concludes that draught animals will remain a major source of power and recommends further methods to contribute towards increasing the profitability of animal traction.

2.57 UZUREAU, C. **Animal Draught in West Africa.** World Crops 26: 112-114. May/June 1974.

Paper dealing with advantages and problems relating to animal draught cultivation in West Africa based on information and statistics from 1972 from three countries, Senegal, Mali and Dahomey. Concludes that even with the constraints of dry season food shortage, shortage of implements, lack of suitable credit facilities and extension services and a predominant system of shifting cultivation which must be stabilised to introduce animals, animal draught is still making considerable progress. Concludes that while research is still under way into different and 'higher' power inputs a more widespread use of draught animals is one of the most effective ways of assisting the development of agriculture in the semi arid areas of West Africa.

2.58 VILLEGAS, V. **The Role of Work Animals in the Philippines.** Animal Husbandry Agriculture Journal, 6 (7): 6 1971.

2.59 WAGNER, C.M.; MUNZINGER, P. **Introduction of Draught Animals in North West Cameroon by the Wum Area Development Authority.** Part C/1 in 'Animal Traction in Africa' compiled by P. Munzinger, G.T.Z., 1982.

Looks at locational and socioeconomic conditions for the use of draught animals, at the history and development of the WADA project, the experience gained to date with the draught animal programmes and evaluates the use of animal in the Wum area. Concludes that although experience is not yet sufficient to permit definitive statements concerning, for example, the profitability of the use of draught animals, the programme as a whole can be considered a success. The fact that draught animals are now being used by farmers who previously made use of the opportunties for subsidised tractor work provides proof of the superiority of draught animals over other more 'advanced' forms of mechanisation.

2.60 WRIGHT, P. **Integrated Programme for Technical Change.** In Report of the Rural Technology Meet for East, Central and Southern Africa, 1977, Commonwealth Secretariat.

Hypothesis, technology, be it appropriate or not, is not the sole answer to adoption. Outlines 6 stages which should be passed through to the introduction of a new technology; a) The analysis of needs, resources and constraints, b) Search for suitable existing equipment, c) Design, construction and testing of prototypes, d) Field testing of prototypes, e) Limited adoption, f) Widespread adoption. special attention should be given to a) Giving enough time, b) Technology for whose needs? Points to a lack of effective coordination between the organisations concerned with supplies of inputs (finance, training, markets, repair, maintenance etc.).

3 The Technology of Animal Draught Use

3.1 Tillage Techniques, Implements and Harnessing

3.1.1 ALI, I. **Bullock Power and Implements for Small and Marginal Farmers.** Allahabad Farmer, 48 (1): 73-80 1977.

3.1.2 AREMU, J.A. **Effects of Different Cultivation Techniques on Infiltration.** In Proceedings of the Appropriate Tillage Workshop, I.A.R., Zaria, Nigeria, 16-20 January 1979, Commonwealth Secretariat.

Compares tractor ox and hand cultivation for effects on infiltration. Tractors appear to be most problematic.

3.1.3 ASTATKE, A.; MATTHEWS, M.D.P. **1981 Progress Report of the Cultivation Trials and Related Cultivation Work at Zebre Ziet and Debre Berhan.** I.L.C.A. Highland Programme Report, 1982.

Report summarising results of research station trials and studies to evaluate three cultivation systems, traditional plough, mouldboard plough and modern spring tine, in relation to three major crops through a comparison of cultivation and weeding times, power requirement and final crop yields.

3.1.4 ALI, N.; PATRA, S.K.; LALL, R.R. **Catalogue of Improved Agricultural Tools, Implements and Equipment in India.** Central Institute of Agricultural Engineering (I.C.A.R.) Bhopal, India, 1979.

Agricultural tools and implements developed and available in India are described individually under the following headings; function, specifications, where developed, test results (suitability for crops and soils, work rate, labour requirements), approximate cost, general information and address of manufacturer in India.

3.1.5 BARTON, D; JEANRENAUD, J.P. **Alternative Technologies for Agricultural Production.** Undergraduate Dissertation (1981), School of Development Studies, University of East Anglia, Norwich, England.

A discussion of high technology agricultural production, contrasted with alternative organic, zero and minimum tillage techniques. An appraisal of the political and socioeconomic implications of technology transfer with reference to selected past and present prospects in tropical agriculture and the relevance of alternative technologies in both developed and less developed countries with particular emphasis on draught bovine power.

Presents experimental results showing the viability of draught oxen as an on-farm power source given a model unit size of approximately 15-20 acres.

3.1.6 BARTON, D.; JEANRENAUD, J.P,; GIBBON, D. **An Animal Drawn Toolcarrier for Small Farm Systems.** Discussion Paper No. 110, School of Development Studies, U.E.A., Norwich, England (1982).

Description of a low cost animal drawn tool carrier developed by the authors for use on the School of Development Studies Rural Technology Unit. Diagrams and photographs are included with costings of the equipment.

3.1.7 BARWELL, I.; AYRE, M. **The Harnessing of Draught Animals.** Intermediate Technology Publication 1982. Prepared by Intermediate Technology Transport Ltd., Ardington, Oxon., OX12 8PN.

Information paper covering harnessing principles (draught characteristics of bovines and equines, requirements of efficient harnesses), bovine harnesses (describes and analyses traditional bovine yokes and presents information on improved technologies), and equine harnesses (describes and analyses existing harnesses and presents information and designs suited to developing country conditions).

3.1.8 BINSWANGER, H.P.; GHODAKE, R.D.; THIERSTEIN, G.E. **Observations on the Economics of Tractors, Bullocks and Wheeled Toolcarriers in the Semi Arid Tropics of India.**

SEE ENTRY 1.10

3.1.9 BLOOM, R.A. **A Review of Technical Evidence on the use of Animal Traction in Sahelian Farming Systems.** Ph.D Dissertation, Michigan State University, U.S.A., 1979.

3.1.10 BOSHOFF, W.H.; MINTO, S.D. **Energy Requirements and Labour Bottlenecks and Their Influence on the Choice of Improved Equipment.**

SEE ENTRY 1.12

3.1.11 BOYD, J.E.L. **Animal Drawn Earth Moving Equipment.** Intermediate Technology Development Group (I.T.D.G.) Agriculture Unit 1980.

Catalogue of various earth movers with details of manufacturers.

3.1.12 BOYD. J.E.L. **Tools for Agriculture : A Buyers Guide to Low Cost Agricultural Implements.** Intermediate Technology Publications Ltd., 9 King Street, London, WC2E 8HN.

Describes commercially manufactured small farm implements which are available for use in developing countries and gives details of manufacturers. Contains information on hand operated, animal drawn and small engine powered equipment in sections classified by types of farming operations.

3.1.13 BOYD, J.E.L.; AYOK, E.A. **Report on Farm Equipment Development Project Daudawa, N.C.S. Nigeria. November 1971 - December 1973.** I.T.D.G. 1974.

Report on project concerned with design, development, production and use of farm equipment at a technological level identified by surveys. Details of equipment are given, with a discussion of local manufacturing considerations. Concludes with recommendations for future projects.

3.1.14 BRUMBY, P.J.; SINGH, K. **India: Animal Powered Agriculture and Improved Technology, An Interim Report.** Report to the World Bank (I.B.R.D.), Washington D.C., U.S.A. 1981.

Intent of report is to summarise present information on the type of and performance of the animal drawn implements available in India, to assess the impact that any 'improved' versions of these implements might have on agricultural output, and to identify possible means of improving the utilisation and efficiency of the draught animal - equipment complex. Concludes that toolbar carriers offer greatest promise, and that improved seed and fertiliser drills adapted to use with the traditional plough appear likely to have a major impact on crop productivity.

3.1.15 CHALMERS, G.R.; MARSDEN, R.H. **Animal Drawn Equipment for Tropical Agriculture.** Journal of Agricultural Engineering Research, 7 (3): 254-257 1962.

Details of an animal drawn toolframe designed by the National Institute for Agricultural Engineering with an account of field trials of the equipment in East Africa.

3.1.16 CHAM, P. **Appropriate Tillage Systems Evaluation by the Department of Agricultural Engineering in the Gambia.** In Proceedings of the Appropriate Tillage Workshop, I.A.R., Zaria, Nigeria, 16-20 January 1979 (a) Commonwealth Secretariat. (Senior Agricultural Engineer, Yundum Experimental Station, The Gambia).

Review of trials in the Gambia with various types of implements to determine the most suitable animal drawn package for crop production. Results of implement performance are given, the Sine hoe package being selected as most suitable.

3.1.17 CHAM, P. **The Use of Appropriate Technology in Gambian Agriculture.** In Report of the West African Rural Technology Meeting, 14-22 May 1979. (b) Commonwealth Secretariat.

Outlines appropriate technology and reviews government policy and reasons for failure of the Emcot ridger and Aplos toolframe. Gives good adoption rates for the Sine hoe.

3.1.18 CHITEDZE FARM MACHINERY INVESTIGATION SECTION **A Comparison of Four Types of Ox Drawn Planters.** Report No. 70/6 1972, Chitedze Agricultural Research Station, P.O. Box 158, Lilongwe, MALAWI.

Four planters are described and compared; a) N.I.A.E. 'sisis' soft roller seeder, b) N.I.A.E. notched wheel seeder, c) Unibar combined planter. The most promising was found to be the N.I.A.E. soft roller 'sisis' seeder.

3.1.19 DUNHAM, R.J. **Cultivation Experiments with Zero Tillage at I.A.R., Zaria**

SEE ENTRY 1.19

3.1.20 EVALUATION OF FARMING SYSTEMS AND AGRICULTURAL IMPLEMENTS PROJECT. (E.F.S.A.I.P.) BOTSWANA. **Animal Draught Systems Study.** Report No. 1 November 1977, Ministry of Agriculture, Division of Agricultural Research, ARS Sebele, Gaberone, BOTSWANA.

Report of first years work of E.F.S.A.I.P. Aims at subsistence farming systems. Project is designed to test new farming systems and equipment in comparison with traditional methods of crop production. Three systems were tested; a) AMP system, using existing implements, b) Versatool toolcarrier (designed by the D.F.R.S. - see entry 4.3.1.31), c) makgonatsotlhe system, a locally produced toolcarrier (see entry 4.3.1.44). Engineering information on the toolcarriers is included. Major defects were revealed in both versatool and makgonatsotlhe systems, the AMP system was seen as most satisfactory. There follow conclusions and recommendations.

3.1.21 E.F.S.A.I.P. (BOTSWANA) **Animal Draught Systems Study - Agricultural Engineering.** Report No. 4 1979-80 (as above).

Report on trials of four improved crop production systems compared with traditional production system. a) Makgonatsotlhe b) E.F.S.A.I.P., c) SAFIM, d) Plough planting. Results cover rainfall, crop establishment performance of planting method, plant population and yield. An economic analysis of each system with labour and draught requirements are included. Conclusions, recommendations and a full engineering report follow.

3.1.22 ELLMAN, A.; MACKAY, B.; MOODY, T. (eds) **Guide to Technology Transfer In East Central and Southern Africa.** Food Production and Rural Development Division, Commonwealth Secretariat 1981).

Purpose of this guide is to encourage local production of technology and reduce imports. Reviews constraints on local manufacturers, lack of regional trade and each countries trade constraints. Comprehensive catalogue of small scale agricultural equipment and manufacturers in the commonwealth countries of East, Central and South Africa. (Botswana, Kenya, Lesotho, Malawi, Swaziland, Tanzania, Zambia). Also includes the range of implements from the Siscoma factory, Senegal. The range of equipment includes implements for cultivation, harrowing, weeding, planting, harvesting, winnowing, milling, irrigation, power, transport. Guide prices (as at May 1st 1980) are given in local currency and U.S. $ equivalent.

3.1.23 FARM MACHINERY RESEARCH UNIT (ZAMBIA) **Manufacture and Introduction of Hand and Animal Drawn Implements.** Project No. 4, Regional Appropriate Technology Programme, F.M.R.U., Department of Agriculture, Magoye, Zambia.

SEE ENTRY 2.9

3.1.24 F.M.R.U. (ZAMBIA) **Ox and Hand Operated Machinery.** Reports No.s 1-9 January 1980. Reginal Research Station, P.O. Box 11. Magoye, Zambia.

Description, background, field test details and conclusions for ox drawn and hand operated machinery. a) Northland No. 5 Cultivator (ox drawn), b) Northland No. 4 Mouldboard ridger (ox drawn), c) Navel bellows knapsack sprayer (hand operated), d) Tencoma T, ULV sprayer (hand operated), e) Tencoma T12P sprayer (hand operated), f) MDM No. 1 and No. 2 Harrows (ox drawn), g) Magoye/Unza groundnut lifter (ox drawn), h) ZNZ spike hoe (hand operated), i) ZNS spike hoe (hand operated).

3.1.25 FISCHER, R.C. **A More Efficient Buffalo Plough.** Agricultural Mechanisation in Asia, Africa and Latin America. 13 (3): 11-14 1982.

Farmers who cannot afford engine power require means for improving their output by increasing their timeliness of field operations. A reduction of approximately one third in the specific draught requirement was obtained in controlled tests compared to a typical manufacturers plough for the N.W. region of Thailand. The improvement was obtained with a larger radius of curvature, a change in orientation of the plough relative to the soil and a reduction in the point suction angle.

3.1.26 FOSTER, J.D.G. **Design of Animal Drawn Planters for Semi Arid Conditions.** Final Scientific Report of Phase 11, Volume 4 1980, Dryland Farming Research Scheme (DFRS) Botswana. Ministry of Agriculture, Division of Agricultural Research, ODA Project R3045.

Animal drawn planters are evaluated to determine the best design for simple planter for the semi arid conditions of Botswana. The results of field tests are discussed and recommendations for official policy farming practice, design of planters and for further research are presented.

3.1.27 FROESE, C. **Harness Project Report.** July 1980 Mochudi Farmers Brigade, Kgaleng Development Board, P.O. Box 208, Mochudi, Botswana.

Maintains that better harnessing increases efficiency. Describes and discusses different types of harnesses for donkeys and oxen.

3.1.28 GIBBON, D. **Dryland Crop Production in Botswana.** A Review of Research 1969-1974, Government Printer, Gabarone, Botswana. (1974).

Physical review of an agricultural system. a) Crop production technique tillage, b) Implements - improved and traditional, c) Design of improved crop production system, d) Implications and adoption, bearing in mind custom, labour and environment.

3.1.29 GIBBON, D; HARVEY, J; HUBBARD, K. **A Minimum Tillage System for Botswana.** World Crops 26 (5) : 229-234 September/October 1974. Also available as Development Studies Reprint, No. 5, University of East Anglia, Norwich.

Discussion of production problems in Botswana which require improvement in the methods practised by farmers, involving several radical changes. A farming system devised in response to this need by the Dryland Farming Research Scheme is outlined and an animal drawn toolcarrier designed and constructed by the authors as an integral part of the production system is described. (the Versatool - see entry 4.3.1.31).

3.1.30   GIBBON, D.; HESLOP, C.; HARVEY, J. **The Hashasha and Atulba Toolbar.** Discussion Paper No. 21 1978, School of Development Studies, University of East Anglia, Norwich, England.

Broad work involving a study of present systems (economic and social, climate and soils etc.) and an attempt to produce a toolbar with local constrints in mind, resulting in the Hashasha weeder and Atulba toolbar.

3.1.31   GOPLAND, S. **Bullock Drawn Groundnut Digger.** Indian Farming, 11 (11): 55-67 1970.

3.1.32   GOPLAND, S.; ANANTHARAMAN, S.E. **Bullock Drawn Potato Digger.** Indian Farming, 11 (11): 36-37 1970.

3.1.33   HOPFEN, H.J. **Farm Implements for Arid and Tropical Regions.** Food and Agriculture Organisation, Agricultural Development Paper No. 91 1969.

Comprehensive global review of implements and equipment for animal draught and hand cultivation.

3.1.34   HUBBARD, K.; HARVEY, J.; GIBBON, D. **The Versatool - An Animal Drawn Toolcarrier for Crop Production Systems in Semi Arid Regions.** Dryland Farming Research Scheme (DFRS) Technical Bulletin No. 6 1974. Botswana Ministry of Agriculture, Division of Agricultural Research. (ODA Research Project R2 2420).

Description, drawings, specifications and photographs of an animal drawn two wheeled implement carrier designed by the DFRS in Botswana for use in an integrated farming system. (see entry 4.3.1.28).

3.1.35   HUSSAIN, A.A.M.; HUSSAIN, M.D.; HOSSAIN, M.M. **Design and Development of Neckharnesses for Cattle in Bangladesh.** Agricultural Mechanisation Asia, 1980.

Low power developed in cattle in Bangladesh is due to poor health of the animals and poor designs of yokes in use. Suggests need to improve the quality of the animals by cross breding and improve draught power by better harness design. Gives criteria of a good yoke and presents the results of experiments using three different types of harnesses.

3.1.36   INTERMEDIATE TECHNOLOGY DEVELOPMENT GROUP. **Agricultural Green Leaflets.** (1973-1976) Intermediate Technology Publications Ltd., 9 King Street, London, WC2E 8HN.

Plans of tools designed for agricultural conditions in Africa intended for distribution to experienced agricultural engineers in the field. Often brief descriptive text. Consisting mainly of construction details and dimensional drawings. Series includes:

1) **The 'Wananchi' ox cart.** Developed at T.A.M.T.U., Tanzania. Built to carry a load of 1400 lbs (636 kg) pulled by two oxen. Wood block and bearing design facilitate ease of maintenance and renewal of bearings by carpenters in rural areas.

2) **Cart for one Draught Animal.** (T.A.M.T.U., Tanzania) Designed to carry a load of 700 lbs (318 kg) pulled by single ox or donkey.

5) **Chitedze Ridgemaster Toolbar.** (origin, Malawi) Locally built and repairable steel plough ridger and cultivator.

4) **Kabanyolo Tolbar.** Locally built steel plough also functioning as a cultivator/weeder.

6) **Prototype Multipurpose Ox Drawn Tool.** (origin Nigeria)

8) **Triangular Spike Tooth Harrow.** (origin India) Teeth made of wood and mild steel, with variable tooth spacing.

9) **Flexible Peg Tooth Harrow and Rigin Frame 'Japanese' Harrow.** Peg tooth harrow designed in Iran. Low cost implement for animal or tractor power, self cleaning. Japanese harrow, simple rigis two row harrow, teeth spaced 6" apart in each row, operates with a cutting action.

10) **Two Designs for Clod Crushers.** (origin Malawi) Simple and cheaply constructed implement used for reducing the size of clods in cultivated land prior to ridging. Made principally of 'gum' (eucalyptus species) poles.

11) **Ox Drawn Tie Ridger/Weeder Implement** (origin Malawi) Attachment designed for use with the 'emcot' ox drawn ridging plough.

12) **IDC Weeding Attachment for EMCOT Plough.** (origin Nigeria) Enables weeding in ridged row crops to be carried out by animal power instead of by hand. Can be adjusted for height and width. Essentially consists of two steel blades pulled along through earth on the side of the ridges.

14) **Sled Type Corrugator/Irrigation Furrow Former** (origin U.S.D.A. Soil Conservation Service) Function is to make small furrows of corugations for water distribution over a field to be used after broadcast seeding or before row crop planting. Can be modified in size to suit animal or tractor draught.

17) **Multiaction Paddy Field Pudding Tool.** (origin Japan) Photoprints only supplied, ox drawn implement.

31) **IT Expandable Cultivator.** (origin Nigeria) Lightweight cultivator designed for weeding of crops planted 70-90 cm spaced rows in sandy soils to be pulled by one or two oxen or donkeys. Adjustable depth and width, suitable for flat ridge cultivation.

33) **High clearance rotary hoe.** Animal drawn implement designed for seeding of crops grown on ridges at 75-90 cm spacing. Not suitable for hard soil conditions but can be used in wet soil.

36) **The Weeder - Mulcher.** (origin India) Animal drawn self cleaning weeder designed to destroy weeds, leave mulch on soil surface and give a high work output per day. Can be used on most crops with a spacing of 30 inches. Easily replaceable blades.

3.1.37 JOHNSON, B.F. AND MUCHIRI, G. **Equipment and Tillage Innovations for Small Scale Farms in Kenya Some Unanswered Questions.** Working Paper No. 197 Institute of Development Studies, University of Nairobi. (1974).

Paper formulates some important and unanswered questions related to choice of equipment and tillage innovations. Aimed at overcoming constraints to increased productivity in dryland farming through the efficient use of animal power. The focus is on innovations capable of easing the seasonal bottlenecks which tend to reduce crop yields because of late planting, and on equipment/tillage systems that will reduce runoff and increase infiltration of the limited rainfall that is recieved in semi arid areas.

3.1.38 JOHNSON, B.F. AND MUCHIRI, G. **Equipment and Tillage Innovations for Kenyas Medium Potential (Semi Arid) Farming Regions.** In Proceedings of a Workshop on Farm Equipment Innovations for Agricultural Development and Rural Industrialisation. Occasional Paper No. 16, 1975, Institute of Development Studies, University of Nairobi, KENYA.

Summarises the information and suggestions received in response to earlier paper (see above). Principle problems that need to be overcome or minimised are

described in general terms. Identifies priority
needs for tillage and equipment innovations in
relation to six problem areas; a) Seedbed
preparation and weed control, b) Seeding and
Planting, c) Soil and moisture conservation
techniques, d) Technique for handling, training and
maintaining draught animals, e) Effective
utilisation of mechanical power currently available,
f) Crop production innovations.

3.1.39 KEMP, D.C. **Development of a New Animal Drawn Tool Carrier Implement for Dryland Tillage.** C.E.E.M.A.T. Technical Meeting 11, March 1980, Section 2.1 'Tillage with Tine Implements - Possible Applications in Hot Countries.' (Overseas Division, N.I.A.E., Silsoe, Bedford, U.K.).

The current development of a new low cost animal
drawn wheeled tool carrier implement for tillage,
planting and transport in dryland agriculture is
reported. The overall design concept, the reasons
for the inclusion of certain features and the
omission of others are discussed. A broad bed
system of cultivation, being developed by
I.C.R.I.S.A.T., for which the toolcarrier is
appropriate is described.

3.1.40 KHEPAR, S.D.; KAUSAL, M.P.; SINGH, M. **The Animal Drawn Lift Irrigation Pump.** Technical Bulletin, March 1982, Department of Soil and Water Engineering, College of Agricultural Engineering, Punjab Agicultural University, Ludhiana 141004, INDIA.

Bulletin containing detailed technical drawing of
animal drawn lift irrigation pump developed during
1974-75 and tested at various centres of I.C.A.R and
in the farmers fields where it has proved quite
successful. Includes a review of various indigenous
animal power water lifting devices used in India, a
description of the design of each component of the
new equipment, an inventory of material required for
pump construction and a performance report covering
efficiency, economic analysis, maintenance, repair
and likely problems with remedies.

3.1.41 LAWRENCE, P. **A Collar for an Ox or Buffalo made from a Worn Out Car or Lorry Tyre.** Centre for Tropical Veterinary Medicine, University of Edinburgh, U.K.

Method of construction of low cost D.I.Y. ox
collar.

3.1.42 LIPPITZ, K. **Fundamental Aspects of Ecology and Crop Growing Relevant to the Use of Draught Animals.** Part B/111 in 'Animal Traction in Africa', compiled by P. Munzinger, G.T.Z., 1982.

Discussion of framework conditions relating to ecology and crop growing which play a part in the use of draught animals in the tropics and subtropics with an emphasis on draught oxen. Covers operations such as land clearance, soil tillage, soil conservation measures, cultivation techniques, weed control and pasture maintenance with a high degree of simplification to cover a wide diversity of situations.

3.1.43 LOWE, P. **Animal Powers as a Complementary Use of Draught Animal Power.** Paper Presented at the Expert Consultation on Appropriate Use of Animal Energy in Agriculture in Africa and Asia. F.A.O., Rome, 1982. (Consultant, G.T.Z., Germany).

Defines the term 'animal powers' (AP's) as every kind of technical equipment which makes use of draught animal power for other purposes than soil tilling and transportation. Possible applications for AP's are water lifting, grinding and crushing, oil pressing, sugar cane cowling, hay baling, chaff cutting, threshing etc. Argues that the use of draught animals for transport and in AP's, as well as for soil tillage would improve the economics of DAP as a whole. Includes a discussion of several aspects connected with the use of AP's.

3.1.44 MACKAY, B. **Rural Technology in the Commonwealth - A Directory of Organisations.** Food Production and Rural Development Division, Commonwealth Secretariat (1980).

Revised edition of 'The Directory of Appropriate Technology Institutions in the Commonwealth' (1977). Concentrates on rural technologies and lists national and international organisations alphabetically by country, with detailed accounts of recent work carried out and publications available from the organisations. Index of equipment and processes, with entries for animal power.

3.1.45 MATTHEWS, M.D.P; PULLEN, D.W.M. **Cultivation and Ox Drawn Implements.** Technical Bulletin No. 1, 1976, Department of Agriculture, The Gambia. (Overseas Department, N.I.A.E., Silsoe, Bedford, U.K.).

Outlines cultivation requirements and recommended practices and lists (with illustration) the range of implements available to farmers in The Gambia.

3.1.46 MATTHEWS, M.D.P.; PULLEN, D.W.M. **Cultivation Trials with Ox Drawn Implements using N'dama Cattle in The Gambia.** Report Series, Tropical Agricultural Engineering Information, N.I.A.E., Silsoe. Reprinted in The Agricultural Engineer, Autumn 1977.

Technical analysis of various implements' efficiency, cost and adaptability to a variety of tasks. Yield per hectare and man hours spent are taken as the measure of success.

3.1.47 MICHAEL, A.M.; KNIERIM, S.C.; REESER, R.M. **Simple Bullock Drawn Implements for Efficient Irrigation.** University of Udaipur, India, 1964.

3.1.48 MOCHUDI FARMERS BRIGADE (BOTSWANA). **The Mochudi Toolbar, 'Makgonatsotlhe' - The Machine Which Can Do Everything.** Agricultural Information Service, Ministry of Agriculture, Gabarone, BOTSWANA, 1975.

The use of the Mochudi toolbar, an animal drawn two wheeled toolbar to which can be attached a planter, fertiliser applicator, disc tillers, sweeps or a standard mouldboard plough, and which can also be used as a carrier when all implements are removed, is described with photographs and line drawings included.

3.1.49 MUCHIRI, G. **Development of Tillage and Equipment Systems in Kenya.** In Proceedings of the Appropriate Tillage Workshop, I.A.R., Zaria, Nigeria, 16-20 January 1979. Commonwealth Secretariat (Department of Agricultural Engineering, University of Nairobi, Kenya).

Report of tillage equipment trials in semi arid Kenya to find a dryland farming tool to replace the traditional mouldboard plough. Results of field efficiency, field capacity, depth of ploughing, draught, surface roughness and soil moisture are given. Concludes suggesting a combination of desi plough and ariana toolbar. Equations for draught related to soil and implement parameters are also given.

3.1.50 MUCHIRI, G. **Effect of Farm Equipment Innovations on Production and Employment in Semi Arid Kenya.** Report to I.L.O. 1978.

Report on tillage and equipment trials to establish the scientific basis for replacing the traditional victory mouldboard plough with a proper dryland farming tool, chisel and 'A' share tines on the Ariana toolbar. In addition two methods of weeding (hand and ox) were included in the trials which were designed to establish the relative advantage of the equipment innovations in terms of soil moisture, dry matter, growth, yield, rate of work, energy requirements, ease of operation and labour requirements.

3.1.51 MUCHIRI, G. **Farm Equipment Innovations for Kenya: An Experimental Approach.** In 'Farm Equipment Innovations in Eastern Africa' (eds) Ahmed and Kinsey, 1981.

Looks at local equipment needs, and tests through to farmer acceptance trials. Concludes that the main limitation is the lack of bullock power. Suggests a package of chisel shares, desi plough and 'A' shares on the Sine hoe toolbar.

3.1.52 MUKOLWE, M. AND MUCKLE, B. **The Purpose and Method of Testing Procedures Carried out at the Agricultural Testing Unit at Nakaru, Kenya.** In Report of the West Africa Rural Technology Meeting, Yundum, The Gambia, and Dakar, Senegal, 14-22 May 1979. Commonwealth Secretariat (A.M.T.U. Box 470, Nakaru, Kenya).

Wherever consideration is being given to the introduction of new equipment or techniques it is essential to reduce the risk of their unsuitability to a minimum through proper evaluation. Discusses the factors to be considered; technical performance, economic factors and the human factor. Comments are given on the reasons behind testing techniques developed at A.M.T.U. for traction and animal drawn equipment. Guidelines for testing procedures are also given.

3.1.53 MUSA, H.L. **Traditional Tillage Operations and Development and Use of Animal Drawn Equipment.** In Proceedings of the Appropriate Tillage Workshop, I.A.R., Zaria, Nigeria, 16-20 January 1979. Commonwealth Secretariat. (Department of Agricultural Engineering, I.A.R. Nigeria).

Review of traditional tillage and cropping practices in Nigeria with discussion of the development, testing and usage of animal drawn equipment (Uniobar, Emcot) and the development of a straddle row rotary weeder.

3.1.54 OGBORN, J.E.A. **Straddle Ridge Cultivation and Equipment for the Heavy Lands of the African Savanna.** In Proceedings of the Appropriate Tillage Workshop, I.A.R., Zaria, Nigeria, 16-20 January 1979. Commonwealth Secretariat. (Department of Agronomy, I.A.R., Nigeria).

Review of research into animal power cultivation in the wetter Guinea zone with heavier soil texture. Ridge cultivation is proposed and the development of the straddle ridge unit is described. An outline of operations worked out to maximise the output of the toolbar is given followed by preliminary experimental results on cotton cultivation. Concludes that the introduction of straddle row weeders halves the post emergent labour requirements and the provision of a tine to cultivate the top of the ridge further reduces labour requirements and increases cotton yields.

3.1.55 OREV, Y. **Improved Farming System for Botswana.** Appropriate Technology, 4 (2) 1977.

Review of suggested improvements in agricultural methods including; manuring, winter fallow, row planting, thinning, improved varieties, harvesting, stubble collection, threshing, harness and draught power.

3.1.56 OREV, Y. **Improving Single Furrow Animal Ploughing in Botswana.** World Crops, November/December 1976, pp 252-253.

Outline of practices in a new system based on the single furrow plough, using reduced numbers of oxen and more efficient harnessing (collar rather than yoke).

3.1.57 PATHAK, B.S. **Selection and Application of Draught Animal Equipment.** Working Paper No. 14, Expert Consultation on Appropriate use of Animal Energy in Agriculture in Africa and Asia. F.A.O., Rome, 15-19 November 1982 (Punjab Agricultural University, Ludhiana, India).

Review of draught animal equipment for; land shaping, tillage, seeding, intercultural operation, chemical application, irrigation, harvesting, transport, yokes and harnesses. Gives table of information on the draught output and hourly cost of operations for some of the improved animal drawn implements. Discusses factors which determine the selection of equipment; land conditions, soils, weeds, crop requirements, water management practices and timeliness and looks at practical problems in the selection of equipment.

3.1.58 PEACOCK, J.M. ET AL. **The Report of the Gambia Ox Ploughing Survey.** Wye College, University of London, U.K. 1966.

3.1.59 PETER, E.C.; PAUL, C.V. **A Bullock Drawn Water Lift for Deep Wells.** Indian Farming 15 (2): 11-12 1967. (Allahabad Agricultural Institute, Allahabad).

A discussion of results of work on the design and construction of the bullock drawn deep well triplex pump initiated by the agricultural engineering department of the Allahabad Agricultural Institute, India, to replace inefficient and outdated indigenous lifts. Describes the mechanism of the lift, testing of the pump and the technical particulars. Although maintenance requirements are lower one of the drawbacks of the pump is its high initial cost.

3.1.60 RAMASWAMY, N.S. **The Management of Animal Resources and the Modernisation of the Bullock Cart System.** Indian Institute of Management, Bangalore, 1979.

Looks at the history of animal drawn cart, technical and infrastructural defects and disadvantages of traditional bullock cart system. Discusses appropriateness of sytem and attemps a modernisation. Moves on to broader issues of animal energy resources in India; improved transmission efficiency, improved implement design, improved breeds of cattle, increased working life of the animal and the problem of cruelty.

3.1.61 RAO, P.S. **Comparative Studies of Some Indian Ploughs with Dynomometers.** Indian Journal of Agricultural Science, 14 (4): 398-433 1944.

3.1.62 SCOTT, D. **Animal Power Boosts New Crop Production.** Appropriate Technology 2 (1): 7-9 1975.

The main obstacle to progress in introducing alternative crops to remote areas dependent on the production for cash of cannabis and opium is the lack of mechanical energy for use with associated machines needed for efficient processing of a greater quantity of farm produce. It is believed that a breakthrough could be achieved with a modern adaptation of an animal power gear unit, which works on the principle of transferring the animals slow movements into the fast rotation of a wheel. The output is partially dependent on the number and strength of the animals used but is usually sufficient for operating a variety of processing machines such as a thresher, grinding mill, chaff cutter or oil press. The article discusses the design, construction and operation of the basic unit which was made in Poland. Major advantages are the low cost of production, minimal operation and maintenance requirements and the fact that it operates on simple and generally well known principles. Examples of the equipment are set up for demonstration at the Laboratoire de Technique Agricoles et Horticoles de Chatelaine, near the European headquarters of the U.N.

3.1.63 SEAGER, A. **Farm Power and Farm Implements in West Pakistan.** World Crops December 1966.

Discussion of traditional animal powered implements in West Pakistan compared to the equivalent or near equivalent motorised ones. Concludes that many of the traditional implements have features vital to the prevailing environmental conditions and that careless replacement of these could do serious damage.

3.1.64 SHULMAN, R. **Strategy for the Advancement of Animal Traction** in **Mali.** Report to U.S.A.I.D., Mali and the Division de Machinisme Agricole June-October 1979. Contract No. 688-79-514. (Department of Crop Science, California Polytech State University, San Luis Obispo, C.A. 93401 U.S.A.).

Study provides technical information from the fields of agronomy, agricultural engineering and animal science relevant to programmes to improve animal traction in Mali. The high labour requirement for weed control is the greatest constraint on the expansion of total cultivated areas. It can be reduced by improved equipment for sowing in rows, for controlling weeds closer to the crop plants and for greater frequency in interrow cultivation. Possible improvements in soil preparation and weed control are discussed.

3.1.65 STARKEY, P.; VERHAEGHE, H. **Weed Control Using Draught animals.**

SEE ENTRY 1.53

3.1.66 SWAMY RAO, A.A. **Local Manufacture and Industrial Equipment in Developing Countries.** In Report on Rural Technology Meet for East, Central and Southern Africa. Commonwealth Secretariat, 1977.

Review of need of less developed countries to produce more of their own agricultural machinery. Proposals on how to promote a production industry.

3.1.67 SWAMY RAO, A.A. **A Report of the Preliminary Investigations, Design, Development and Testing and Economic Analysis of the New Single and Double Bullock Harness at the Allahabad Agricultural Implement and Power Development Centre.** Allahabad Agricultural Institute, India, May 1962-April 1964.

3.1.68 VARMA, S.R.; BHATAGAR, A.P. **Bullock Drawn Reaper with Engine Operated Cutting Bar.** Indian Farming, 11 (11): 29-31 1970.

3.1.69 VARSHNEY, B.P.; MISHRA, T.N.; KUMAR, A.; SINGH, R.P. **Performance of Harnesses Used for Draught Animals.** Agricultural Mechanisation in Asia, Africa, and Latin America. 13 (3) 15-19 1982.

Five animal harnesses from different regions of Uttar Pradesh were evaluated on the basis of speed, rise in temperature, pulse rate and respiration rate of the animal under four different loads. Full results are presented, concluding that the three most desirable harnesses were the Hill, Local and Improved - in that order, from the standpoint of the animal.

3.1.70 VIEBERG, U. **Basic Aspects of Harnessing and the Use of Implements.** Part B/11 in 'Animal Traction in Africa', compiled by P. Munzinger, G.T.Z., 1982.

Covers traction capacity with approximate figures, harnessing with illustrations and assessment of different type of yokes and harness, and a comprehensive section on implements intended to give an idea of the working methods to be used with draught animals under tropical or subtropical conditions, together with appropriate implements. A further section gives some of the data necessary for estimating working time requirements, and in conclusion some aspects of the maintenance and supply of animal drawn implements are discussed.

3.1.71 WILLCOCKS, T.J. **Animal Drawn Toolbar.** Technical Bulletin No. 2, Tropical Agricultural Enineering Information, Overseas Department, N.I.A.E., Silsoe, U.K.

Details of an animal drawn multiple tool frame and attachments produced by N.I.A.E. for use in Africa.

3.1.72 WILLCOCKS, T.J. **Semi Arid Tillage Research in Botswana.** In Proceedings of appropriate Tillage workshop, I.A.R., Zaria, Nigeria, 16-20 January 1979. Commonwealth Secretariat.

Describes trials undertaken to investigate the tillage energy requirements and their effect on soil porosity, soil moisture and yield, with the objective of finding the optimum tilth for crop production, quantifying necessary energy requirements and specifying a tillage system that can be adopted by the farmer in semi arid areas when related to the time of year and the available draught power. Compares methods of cultivation using tractor and ox drawn implements and presents results of bulk density, soil moisture, energy and yields. Results indicate high value of shallow (100mm) tillage and recommendations are made for a system of tillage using a chisel plough and weeding sweep.

3.2 Draught Capacity, Training, Nutrition and General Management

3.2.1 ACHIYA, S.C.P.; UDUNDO, G. **The Advantages and Disadvantages of the 'Indian Method' of Training and Controlling Oxen.** In Proceedings of a Workshop on Farm Equipment Innovations for Agricultural Development and Rural Industrialisation. Occasional Paper No. 16, 1975, Institute of Development Studies, University of Nairobi, Kenya.

Report on the Bakura ox unit project to demonstrate to farmers the Indian method of training and guiding oxen (using one pair of oxen and 1-2 people rather than the traditional teams of 4 or more oxen and 2-3 people). Discussion of the disadvantages of the system; risk, time consumption in preparation, expense, difficult substitution, limited power, skills needed; and the advantages; timeliness of operations increase in operation through accurate guidence, more land released from grazing, reduction in labour bottlenecks. Concludes that it is possible to increase agricultural production using the new system.

3.2.2 ALEXANDER, E.N. **Increasing the Efficiency of the Traditional Systems of Ox Cultivation.** In Proceedings of a Workshop on Farm Equipment Innovations for Agricultural Development and Rural Industrialisation, Occasional Paper No. 16, 1975, Institute of Development Studies, University of Nairobi, Kenya.

Discusses requirements for increasing the efficiency of ox power; a) Improving the work efficiency of oxen (ox capability) through management, selection, nutrition and training, b) Improving the work efficiency of manpower (farmer adaptability) through training programmes for farmers in better utilisation of oxen and implements, c) Improving the working efficiency of equipment (implement availability) advocating locally produced easily maintained equipment.

3.2.3 ANAND, U.; SUNDARASEN, D. **Crossbred Bullocks can Contribute to Agricultural Operations.** Indian Farming, 24 (5): 27-29 1974.

3.2.4 ANDROMEDAS, J.A.; LEWIS, R.E. **Appropriate Technology, Energetics and Draught Animals.** Paper presented at the Annual Meeting of the American Anthropologist Aassociation, Houston, Texas, U.S.A. 2 December 1977.

3.2.5 BARTLETT, J.; BARRETT, E.M. **Draught Animal Power, Past or Future?** Undergraduate Dissertation 1982, School of Development Studies, University of East Anglia, Norwich, U.K.

General review of DAP (past and present use), including review of literature on nutrition. Calculation of feeding rations for a pair of draught bovines on a Norfolk smallholding, using the results of experimental work carried out at the Centre for Tropical Veterinary Medicine, University of Edinburgh. Analysis of a 5 hectare farm system incorporating the use of a pair of draught bovines, and a discussion of management principles and practices for draught bovines with particular reference to water buffalo. Concludes with recommendations for further research.

3.2.6 BARTLETT, J.; BARRETT, E.M.; GIBBON, D. **Nutrition and Working Efficiency of Draught Bovines on a Norfolk Small Holding.** Discussion Paper No. 127, School of Development Studies, University of East Anglia, Norwich, U.K.

One of a series of discussion papers produced within the School of Development Studies (see entry above). Reviews draught animal feeding needs and systems, presenting field results of a trial undertaken by the authors on the Rural Technology Unit of the School using a pair of draught bovines to test a new feeding system developed at the Centre for Tropical Veterinary Medicine, University of Edinburgh. A brief discussion of management issues relating to nutritional requirements is included.

3.2.7 BARTH, K.M.; WILLIAMS, J.W.; BROWN, G.D. **Digestible Energy Requirements of Working and Non-Working Ponies.** Journal of Animal Science, 44: 585-589 1977.

3.2.8 BARTON, D.; JEANRENAUD, J-P.; GIBBON, D. **The Training and Management of Draught Oxen.** Discussion Paper No. 126, 1982, School of Development Studies, University of East Anglia, Norwich, U.K.

One of a series of discussion papers produced by a small group within the School of Development Studies based on a project undertaken by the authors on a 2 hectare research and training farm at the University of East Anglia from 1978 to 1981. This paper discusses the equipment and training method of a pair of draught bullocks, the draught capacity of various animals and the comparative advantages and disadvantages of major types of harnessing. Concludes that a pair of draught oxen can easily be trained to perform the majority of operations for a small farm system, that the use of DAP will continue to play an important role in agricultural systems in developing countries and that DAP also has a potential role in small farm systems in developed countries.

3.2.9 BHAID, M.U. **Oil Crisis and the Bullock Power on the Farm.** Agriculture and Agroindustries Journal, 8: 26-28 1975 (College of Veterinary Science and Animal Husbandry, Mhow, M-P, India).

Argues that animals should be used more efficiently for work throughout the year. Calculates rations for idle and working bullocks fed on the common feeds available in the Malwa region of Madhya Pradesh (oil cake, wheat straw and maize).

3.2.10 BHATTACHARYA, P. **Investigations on Standardisation of Draught Capacity of Bullocks in India.** In Proceedings of the 7th International Congress of Animal Husbandry, Madrid, Spain. Vol. 8: 141-143 1959.

3.2.11 BOURN, D.; SCOTT, M. **The Successful Use of Work Oxen in Agricultural Development of Tsetse Infected Land in Ethiopia.** Tropical Animal Health and Production, 10: 191-205 1978.

Report on a project on a settlement scheme in an area of West Ethiopia infested with tsetse where a herd of work oxen (450 individuals) has been maintained under the protection of trypanocidal drugs. Paper describes the environmental conditions and the epizootiology of trypanosomiasis in the oxen and in the vector **Glossina Morsitans.** It is concluded that with the strategic use of drugs oxen can be kept alive and perform useful agricultural work in areas of high tsetse challenge, provided reasonable standards of veterinary supervision and management are maintained.

3.2.12 BRODELL, A.P.; JENNINGS, R.D. **Work Performed and Feed Utilised by Horses and Mules.** U.S.D.A. Bureau of Agricultural Economics, Washington D.C. U.S.A.

3.2.13 BRZESKI, E.; MORSTIN, J. **(Studies on the Utility Value of Mules).** Acta. Agrar. Silvest., Ser Zootech 3: 49-58 (Taken from Animal Breeding Abstracts 33: 530; 1965 (Abs. No. 3125).

The aim of the investigations was to ascertain the characteristics of the mule population of Poland and to evaluate the animal as beasts of burden. Data were obtained for 38 mules and 1 hinny. Height at withers was 152 cm in the mules and 120 cm in the hinny (average). Lipitsa, Mazura and Gubbrandschal mares were all suitable for mule production. The results of preliminary tests confirmed the value of the mule as a draught animal in agriculture.

3.2.14 BUHLE, P. **(Evaluation of Pulling Power of the Horse).** Dtsch. Landw. Tierz; 38: 645-647. (From Animal Breeding Abstracts 2: 301; 1934)

Article dealing with conformation and strength of the horse. The author points out that the maximum pull amounts to 70-100% of the body weight as compared with 50% in the case of caterpillar tractors and 15% in a railway engine. Research on inheritance of pulling power in draught horses is desirable.

3.2.15 BURGEMEISTER, R. **(Distribution and Use of Dromedaries)** Tropenlandwirt (1976) 77: 43-53 (Taken from Animal Breeding Abstracts 46: 455; 1978 (No. 4067).)

A review including data from the literature on load bearing ability, speed, hair yield and milk production and composition.

3.2.16 BOWMAKER, R.J. **Using Work Oxen in Malawi.** Extension Aids Branch publication, Department of Ahriculture, Ministry of Economic Affairs, Malawi (1968).

Booklet intended for use by the farmer and field staff. Discusses selection, training and management of work oxen, and implement and equipment use and maintenance.

3.2.17 COCKRILL, W. ROSS. **The Draught Buffalo (Bubalus bubalis).** The Veterinarian 5: 265-272 1968.

An account is given of the various work purposes for which the water buffalo is used. The versatility of the animal is described. There is little evidence of a decline in the stocks of working buffalo as mechanisation extends. The author suggests that buffaloes will not disappear but will be utilised increasingly for meat production.

3.2.18 DEVADATTUM, D.S.K.; MAURYA, N.L. **Draughtability of Hariana Bullocks.** Indian Journal of Dairy Science, 31 (2): 120-127 1978. (Agricultural Engineering Institute, Raichur - 584101, Karnataka, India).

An average pair of Hariana bullocks was tested by hauling a load for 8 cycles, each cycle distance being 375 metres. Parameters such as body temperature and pulse rates of bullocks, atmospheric temperature and relative humidity were recorded. It was found that the atmospheric temperature played a more predominant role in the onset of fatigue in the bullocks compared to load imposed on them. The power input of the bullocks was found to decrease with incresased duration of testing. It was also observed that power output increased with increase in draught but at a slower rate. The optimum draught for an average pair of hariana bullocks was found to be about 60 kg. The correlations between power output, pulse rate and body temperature indicated that higher output causes early onset of fatigue in the bullocks.

3.2.19 DIBBITS, H.J. **Factors Which Influence the Power Output of Draught Animals.** Department of Agricultural Engineering, University of Nairobi, Kenya.

Factors influencing the output of draught animals are discussed; health species, breed, weight, sex, feeding, work environment and training. Attention is also given to different kinds of harnessing.

3.2.20 DUSEK, J. **(Performance Testing with Maximum Loads for Horses).** Zivocisna Vyroba 6 (34): 571-588 (Taken from Animal Breeding Abstracts 30: 17; 1962 (No. 49).)

Conclusions were drawn from tests with 80 horses. Tractive force was found to be related to body weight only in groups in which body weight was clearly differentiated. Exponential equations were used to show the relations between length of pace and tractive force and the decrease in speed with increasing loads. Over 30 km the maximum tractive force was 14-15% of body weight. Of all the horses tested Lipitsas, Kladnibs and the crosses of each with Belgian mares proved the most satisfactory for agricultural work.

3.2.21 DYRENDAHL, S.; BENGTSSON, G. **Performance Testing of Draught Horses: Initiatives and Experience of the North Swedish Horse Association.** Working Paper No. 8, Expert Consultation on the Appropriate Use of Animal Energy in Agriculture in Africa and Asia, F.A.O., Rome, Italy 15-19 November 1982. (College of Veterinary Medicine, The Swedish University of Agricultural Sciences, S-750 07 Uppsala, Sweden).

Report on performance testing of draught horses in Sweden by the N.S.H.A. and the Stallion Rearing Institute at Wangen, through the use of stationary and mobile ergometers and draught aptitude tests at county horse shows. Concludes that complicated power tests in fixed or mobile apparatus will probably never be equal in efficiency and fairness to the simple but sensibly arranged draught aptitude tests judged by skilled and experiences judges.

3.2.22 ELMER, L.A. **Care and Management of Working Oxen.** East African Agricultural Journal 4 (4): 213-220 April 1944.

Deals with class of animals, colour feeding, grazing, shade and shelter, sickness, bloat, constipation, drenching, sore necks, abscesses, broken horns, medicine, training, refusal to work and management.

3.2.23 FENG YANG LIAN **The Use of Draught Cattle in China.**

SEE ENTRY 2.14

3.2.24 FENG YANG LIAN, ET AL. **Study of Feeding Standards of Draught Cattle.** Journal of Chinese Animal Science, July 1963.

3.2.25 FOOD AND AGRICULTURE ORGANISATION OF THE UNITED NATIONS. **Assistance in the Capturing of Wild Buffaloes for Animal Draught Purposes.** F.A.O. 1979.

3.2.26 GOE, M.R.; MCDOWELL, R.E. **Animal Traction: Guidelines for Utilisation.** Cornell International Mimeograph 81 December 1980, Cornell University, Ithaca, New York.

Objective of the paper is to provide a 'state of the art' on the utilisation of animals for traction with a major emphasis on power for agriculture. Covers, a) Definitions of the principles of animal draught (friction, force, speed) and evaluation of the effects on animal performance, b) Draught capacity of animals, c) A survey of animal traction in warm climates, different species used for draught and comparative performances, d) Discussion of nutritive requirements of draught animals.

3.2.27 HALL, J.F. **Notes on Ox Training.** Published by the Ministry of Agriculture, Forests and Wildlife, Dar-es-Salaam.

Pamphlet covering stages of training, general notes on working oxen equipment and implements, with diagrams.

3.2.28 HONZAWA, S.; ISHIZAKI,S.; SHINOHARA, A.; KIYAMA, K. **(Relation Between Size and Work Power in the Horse)** J. Kanto-Tosan Agric. Exp. Sta.; 15: 112-120 (Taken from Animal Breeding Abtracts, 28: 378; 1960 No. 1787)

Correlations between working ability, maximum draught capacity and various body measurements were calculated for adult horses of different sizes. Close correlations were found between body dimensions and most of the criteria of working ability, e.g. the area of paddy field ploughed in four hours. There was also a distinct correlation between body dimensions and maximum pulling power.

3.2.29 HOWARD, C.R. **The Draught Ox Management and Uses.** Zimbabwe Rhodesia Agricultural Journal 77 (1): 19-34 1979.

General discussion covering history of DAP, Zimbabwe indigenous breeds for draught, work capacity, selection, training, yoking and harnessing systems, management and a review of implements.

3.2.30 ILANGANTILEKE, S.G.; JAYATISSA, D.N.; GUPTA, C.P. **The Use and Measurement of Draught Power in Buffaloes.** Paper presented at a Workshop on Water Buffalo Research in Sri Lanka, 24-28 November 1980, Peradeniya, SRI LANKA.

Rearing animals with high draught capabilities is necessary for maximum utilisation of animal power. Measurement of draught in different breeds is a necessary first step in breeding programmes. Details a device to measure the draught power of animals using a calibrated spring type dynomometer. The change in draught power with soil penetration resistance at different moisture contents and the relationship between draught capability and speed of animal was observed during the initial testing stage of the measuring device.

3.2.31 INDIAN COUNCIL OF AGRICULTURAL RESEARCH. **Characteristics of Cattle and Buffalo Breeds in India.** I.C.A.R., New Delhi, INDIA.

3.2.32 INTERNATIONAL LIVESTOCK CENTRE FOR AFRICA. **Trypanotolerant Livestock in West and Central Africa.** Vol. 2, Country Studies, I.L.C.A., Addis Ababa, Ethiopia, 1979.

3.2.33 ISHIZAKI, S.; HONZAWA, S.; SHINIHARA, A.; KOYAMA, K. **Comparison of Working Ability of Cattle and Horses.** J. Kanto-Tosan Agric. Sta. 18: 259-268 (Taken from Animal Breeding Abstracts 23: 123; 1962 No. 1522).

Performance tests carried out on 10 Japanese Black cows and 20 horses. Tests of 4 hours comprised pulling a wagon, ploughing paddy fields with a Japanese plough, carrying a load and pulling a wagon with a maximum load a distance of 600 m. Horses generally superior to cattle in first two tests, no significant difference between cattle and horses in maximum load but ratio between maximum load and body weight averaged 51% in cattle and 43% in horses. Cattle were more stable than horses as pack animals (centre of gravity lower). In fourth test although maximum load and mean draught resistance was less in cattle the ratio of maximum load to body weight was higher.

3.2.34 JEANRENAUD, J-P.; BARTON, D.; GIBBON, D. **Draught Animal Power.** Discussion Paper No.125, December 1982, School of Development Studies, University of East Anglia, Norwich, U.K.

One of a series of papers produced by a small group within the School based on experiences of a project undertaken by the authors in which draught bullocks were used within a small farm system at the University. This paper discusses the historical role of draught animals in agriculture and explores the ox vs. horse debate in the U.K. and in selected areas where draught animals are of major importance today. This is followed by a discussion of the potential value of draught animals particularly in relation to technology options, power availability and energy use within small farm systems. Concludes with suggestions of areas where there may be scope for a more systematic approach to improvement.

3.2.35 KAVISHE, T.S. **The Limitations of Introducing and Multiplying Horses in Tanzania.** Tanzanian Soc. Animal Production Conference, May 26-30, 1981, Arusha, Tanzania.

3.2.36 KRAUTFORST, J.W. **(Influence of Work Balanced by Food on the Efficiency of Cows).** Firzegle. Lodowl 15: 122-129, 196-202 (Taken from Animal Breeding Abstracts 16: 115; 1948 No. 490).

Cows of medium yield (up to 12kg milk) and in good physical condition can stand even all day work (balanced by food) without any considerable influence on milk yield. Work has no effect on the specific gravity of the milk. The initial drop in milk density is due to an increase in the fat content. Heavy work may, however, cause a slight decrease in the yield and percentage of fat. The general health of cows is improved by work, especially that of animals confined to byres. Only young animals (4-7 years) in good condition should be used for draught. In general their use for this is recommended. Any undesirable effects of work are outweighed by its favourable effects.

3.2.37 LALL, H.K. **The Use of Cows for Work.** Indian Farming, 10 (7): 286-287.

3.2.38 MATHERS, J.C. **Nutrition of Draught Animals.** Working Paper No. 13, Expert Consultation on Appropriate Use of Animal Energy in Agriculture in Africa and Asia. F.A.O., Rome, Italy, November 1982. Also C.T.V.M. Mimeo. (Centre for Tropical Veterinary Medicine, University of Edinburgh, U.K.).

This paper looks at nutritional needs of ruminants and equines. Covers energy needs for maintenance, walking, carrying and pulling, with specimen calculations. Constraints on work output are discussed, food intake, disease and climate.

3.2.39 MCDOWELL, R.E. **Importance of Ruminants of the World for Non-Food Uses.** Department of animal science, New York State College of Agriculture and Life Sciences, Cornell University, Ithaca, New York. September 1976.

The world's population of ruminants that man has under full or partial control is about 2.8 billion. In most cultures cattle or other ruminants do not compete with man for agricultural products or land; therefore, no actual or potential agricultural lands are sacrificed in their support. In addition to serving as a large food resource, ruminants provide goods and 'services' of non-food nature which may have economic value equal to or exceeding that of food. Some products such as fibres and inedible byproducts of slaughter are important to world commerce, but others, for which no monetary values are available, are as important or more so to man's needs - traction, animal excreta for fertiliser or fuel, storage of capital, ecological conservation, pest control and cultural preferences, including recreation. About 12% of worlds population is fully or highly dependent on pastoral herding of ruminants. Nearly 50.5 of all farms of the world have some dependence on animal power and there is almost universal dependence on ruminants for transport of goods. While these uses are not presently utilised efficiently, and their potential largely unexplored, clearly humans and ruminants have a much greater interdependence than as a food resource. Recognition that fossil fuels are limiting, and that ecological considerations are important, will lead to expansion of numbers and man's dependence on ruminants.

3.2.40 METTRICK, H.M.; JAMES, D.P. **Farm Power in Bangladesh. Volume 2, Part One. Some Aspects of the Economics of Animal Power. Part Two. Mechanisation and Institutions in Noakhali.**

SEE ENTRY 4.2.25

3.2.41 MUKHERJEE, D.P.; DUTTA, S.; BHATTACHARYA, P. **Studies on the Draught Capacity of Hariana Bullocks.** Indian Journal of Veterinary Science and Animal Husbandry, 31 (39): 39-50 1961.

Reviews past investigations into draughtability of Hariana bullocks in India. Details experimental trials undertaken to find out if the draught capacity of bullocks could be correlated with physiological characteristics of the animals which could easily be measured under field conditions. A discussion of results follows.

3.2.42 NANGIA, O.P.; RANA, R.D.; SINGH, N.; AHMAD, A. **A Note on Draught Capacity in Castrated and Entire Male Buffaloes as Reflected in Some Blood Constituents.** Animal Production 27 (2): 237-240 1978.

There is a general belief among the villagers in the state of Haryana that castration renders male buffaloes less efficient in work capacity, and therefore castration is not practised. This leads to undesirable breeding. A comparison has been made of the physiological response to work in castrated and entire males to confirm or dispel the farmers belief. Buffalo male calves of 2 years of age were made to work by pulling a stone roller weighing 80 kg at a constant speed of about 3 km/hour on even ground for three hours. There was no difference in the concentration of blood constituents of the two groups. It was concluded that castrated and entire male buffaloes reacted in a similar manner to the stress of work.

3.2.43 PATHAK, B.S. **Management and Untilisation of Camels for Work.** Working Paper No. 7, Expert Consultation on Appropriate Use of Animals in Agriculture in Africa and Asia. F.A.O., Rome, 15-19 November 1982. (Punjab Agricultural University, Ludhiana, India.)

A general review of camels as work animals covering all aspects of management; breeds, characteristics, housing, feeding practices, handling and training, health care, work physiology and environmental effects, power output and work capacity, economics and utilisation.

3.2.44 PATHAK, B.S.; GILL, B. **Management and Utilisation of Cattle for Work.** Working Paper No. 5, Expert Consultation on the Use of Animal Energy in Agriculture in Africa and Asia, F.A.O., Rome, Italy, 15-19 November 1982.

A general review of management aspects of DAP covering; background of DAP, draught calttle breeds, feeding practices, housing, training, health care, work physiology, draught and power output, selection of animals and work management and economics of utilisation.

3.2.45 PERDOK, H.B. **Urea Ensiled Paddy Straw and its Potential as Draught Animal Feed.** Paper presented at the Regional Seminar on Farm Power, October 1982, Agrarian Research and Training Institute, Colombo, SRI LANKA.

Animal draught in Sri Lanka is mainly related to the cultivation of paddy. Paddy straw should therefore be considered as an alternative feed source. Experiments using treated straw (method given) on groups of cows and bullocks are described and the results presented. Milk and milk fat yields increased significantly with treated straw and liveweight gains also increased. Suggests that strategic feeding of urea ensiled straw would enable single animal tillage with a dramatic positive impact on the draught poential of the limited stock.

3.2.46 RAMASWAMY, N.S. The Management of Animal Energy Resources and the Modernisation of the Bullock Cart.

SEE ENTRY 3.1.60

3.2.47 RAO, M.V.N. A Comparative Study of the Draught Capacity of Crossbred Bullocks and Indiginous Bullocks. National Dairy Resarch Institute, Karnal, India, Mimeo, 1972.

3.2.48 RAUT, K.C. Working Bullocks: Their Nutritional Status and Utilisation in Some Areas. National Seminar on DAP Systems in India, Bangalore 1982.

3.2.49 REH, I. Animal Husbandry and Veterinary Aspects. Part B/1 in 'Animal Traction in Africa', compiled by P. Munzinger, G.T.Z. 1982.

Covers a wide range of management aspects, the selection and availability of draught cattle in Africa; the time, duration and procedure for training, feeding (giving basic nutrient requirements specified in U.F. and T.D.N. for light, medium or heavy work, mineral requirements and water requirements). This section also includes a useful table showing the nutrient content for selected feedstuffs. Practical aspects of feeding are covered, including grazing, fodder storage, fodder conservation and examples of rations. Hygiene and veterinary aspects of husbandry are discussed, with comments on major diseases, injuries and control methods. A short discussion on marketing follows, with subsections on marketing structure, accessibility of livestock markets, pricing and fattening of cull cattle. In conclusion this paper looks briefly at other types of draught animals with some general comparisons between cattle, horses and donkeys.

3.2.50 RIZWAN-UL-MUQTADIR,; GILL, R.A.; AHMAD, Z.; AHMAD, M. Draught Power and its Effects on Milk Yield and Milk Composition in Lactating Buffaloes in the Winter Season. Pakistan Journal of Agricultural Sciences 12 (1-2): 93-98 1976.

Three matched lactating buffalo cows worked for three hours/day for 21 days. Average area ploughed in 3 hours was 0.57 acres and draught power was 155.3 lbs/buffalo. (i.e. 12.4% of body weight). Work had no significant effect on milk yield or on milk composition.

3.2.51 ROTH, M. AND NORMAN, D. Role of Animals in the Small Farm Enterprise prepared for Integrated Crop and Animal Production and Optimise Resource Utilisation on Small Farms in Developing Countries, The Rockfeller Foundation Conference Center, Bellagio, Italy, October 18-23 1978.

Objective of the paper is to review some of the roles livestock play in ther small farm enterprise; 1) Animal products for food and non-food purposes; 2) Manure as fertiliser and fuel; 3) Animals as a source of power; 4) Livestock as a source of income and a means of saving, investment and economic insurance; 5) Social obligations. A discussion of two levels of integration of livestock and crops, and of the possible improvement of integration; follows concluding that, in order to continue the complementary relationship that traditionally existed between crops and livestock, a different approach to that traditionally used in high income countries is required. Strategies need to be developed **within** the countries, based on an in depth understanding of the local environment, and will need to be more holistic in being compatible not only with the technological, but also with the human elements.

3.2.52 ROY, S.R.; NEOGI, A.K.; GUHA, H. **Cross Bred Bullocks Vs. Indigenous Bullocks for Draught Purposes Under West Bengal Conditions.** Indian Dairyman 24: 66-70 1972.

4 Hariana x Jersey Vs. 4 Hariana averaging 525 and 370 kg respectively used over a 10 day period in 3 ploughing trials. When steers began work at 08.00 hrs the number of hectares/hour ploughed by each team averaged 0.068 with crossbred and 0.053 with purebred on wet land, and 0.040 (crossbred) and 0.0-6 (purebred) on dry. Starting at 06.00 hrs on dryland averaged 0.084 (crossbred) and 0.075 (purebred).

3.2.53 SASIMOWSKI, E. **Breed Improvement of Draught Animals.** Working Paper N. 9, Expert Consultation on the Use of Animal Energy in Agriculture in Africa and Asia, F.A.O., Rome, 15-19 November 1982.

A review of different systems and tests for evaluating the exterior of animals and the characteristics which affect its pulling ability, with proposals for further investigations and undertakings aimed at the improvement of draught animal breeding.

3.2.54 SASIMOWSKI, E. **Management and Utilisation of Equine Animals for Work.** Working Paper No. 4, Expert Consultation on the Use of Animal Energy in Agriculture in Africa and Asia, F.A.O., Rome, 15-19 November 1982.

Compares equines to ruminants for work and discusses problems of feeding and of breeding suitable animals. Lists farming tools and machines used with horses in Poland and concludes with proposals for further research in the following fields; selection of draught animals adapted to prevailing conditions - comparative tests on possibilities of management and draught capabilities of light horses and ponies, of specified breeds; possibilities of producing good hinnies and asses as draught animals on a large scale; possibilities of keeping domestic zebras for draught purposes in Africa and possibilities of meat production from draught horses.

3.2.55 SINGH, D.; SINGH, B.K.; SINGH, R.K. **Use Pattern and Factors of Low Productivity of Draught Animal Power.** National Seminar on DAP Systems in India, Bangalore, 1982.

3.2.56 SIRIWADENE, J.S. DE. S.; WICKREMASURIYA, U.; BALACHANDRAN. **Management Practices of the Buffalo in Small Farms.** Paper presented at a Workshop on Water Buffalo Research in Sri Lanka, November 24-:28 1980, Peradeniya, SRI LANKA.

Results of a survey carried out on the management practices of the water buffalo in smallholdings in the Polomaniwa and Matura districts. Buffaloes are kept for draught and milk production. Covers average size of holdings, milk yields and indicates farmers preference for bulls for ploughing, estimating that a pair of animals can generally plough 0.20 hectares and puddle 0.05 to 0.01 hectares per day.

3.2.57 SITORUS, P.; ZULBARDI, M.; ROESYAT, A. **Performance of Bali Cattle as Work Animals and Milk and Beef Producers.** Indonesian Agricultural Research and Development Journal 1 (1-2): 9-10 1979.

Review of Bali cattle situation, characteristics, exports, reproduction, crossbreeding and feeding practices.

3.2.58 SMITH, A.J. **Draught Animal Research - A Neglected Subject.** World Animal Review 40: 43-48 December 1981.

Article develops the case for animal power, emphasises the need for more research, particularly on basis of nutrituional requirements, harnessing systems and the effects of disease, ambient temperature and under nutrition on work output. Suggests the establishment of an international institute for the subject.

3.2.59 SMITH, A.J. **The Integration of Draught Animals into Agricultural Systems.** Working Paper No. 1, Expert Consultation on Appropriate use of Animal Energy in Agriculture in Africa and Asia, F.A.O., Rome, Italy, 15-19 November 1982. (C.T.V.M., Edinburgh, U.K.).

Argues that in countries where feed supplies for animals are scarce it is important that the animals are integrated fully into farming systems so that they do not compete with humans for food, make the best use of scarce resources available and produce several products so that the maintenance cost of the animal represents a smaller relative tax on each unit of production. Discusses the integration of draught animals into agricultural systems where land is a limiting factor and in systems where land is not limiting. Concludes that more research is needed on the use of draught animals as complete productive unit so that farmers can be advised on how to use them in a more productive way.

3.2.60 SMITH, A.J. **The Role of Draught Animals in Agricultural Systems in Developing Countires.** In 'Vegetable Productivity' (ed) C.R.W. Spedding Institute of Biology, London 1979.

Stresses the importance of animals to world draught. Compares the efficiency of animals and assesses factors affecting numbers of animals needed per 100 hectares. Reviews food consumption and compares animals to hand labour. Concludes by stressing appropriateness of animals and benefits in easing agricultural operations.

3.2.61 TELLEEN, M. **The Draught Horse Primer.** Rodale Press, Emmaus, P.A. 1977.

Argues that draught horses and mules can serve a useful function in todays farms in the U.S.A., especially as the price of farm equipment and fuel increases exponentially. Made up largely of material from booklets in the 1920's and 1930's when heavy horses were the major source of agricultural power, and covers breeding, machinery, harnessing and general management of draught horses.

3.2.62 TORNEDE, H. **(The Problems of Work Performance of Dairy Cows with Special Reference to Red Hill Cattle).** Zuchtungskunde 14: 308-333 (taken from Animal Breeding Abstracts, 8: 230 1954).

80% of Red Hill cattle in Nassam, Hartz, Silesia and Vogtland were used for draught as well as milk and butter production. Conditions of hoof important, 80% of cows shod. Yokes should be replaced by collars. Calculated that 0.6 acres of cultivation requires 11 days (of 8 hours) work per cow per year. Light work stimulates milk production but very heavy work causes a marked decrease (up to 80%). The effects of heavier work may be offset by additional feeding.

3.2.63 TURK, K.L. **Other Roles of Animals, Significance of Animals in Farming Systems and in the Provision of Farm Power and Pleasure.** Cornell University Mimeograph, Ithaca, New York, U.S.A.

4.4 General

4.1 FOOD AND AGRICULTURE ORGANISATION OF THE UNTIED NATIONS.
Manual on the Employment of Draught Animals in Agriculture.
C.E.E.M.A.T 1968. Translated for F.A.O. 1972.

Purpose of manual is to provide information to be used in the preparation and conduct of animal draught operations. Covers most aspects of DAP; Background and present status of animal draught equipment; draught animals available in Africa; choice of animals; care of animals; draught capacity; training; housing; feed requirements and production; harnessing methods; implements; maintenance repair and manufacture of equipment at a local level and economic considerations.

4.2 MUNZINGER, P. **Animal Traction in Africa.** G.T.Z. publication, 1982.

Fairly comprehensive manual with the objective of providing information on the use of draught animals in Africa, based on the hypothesis that DAP is of continuing and increasing importance, supported by shortages and cost of coventional energy and by the need to intensify production in small scale agriculture. The manual is divided into three parts; a) The development and situation of animal traction in Africa and conditions limiting further promotion, b) Basic aspects of the use of draught animals, c) Case studies. Each section and subsection of the manual have been included in the appropriate section of this bibliography as follows;

Development and situation (P. Munzinger)	- 4.2.27
Animal husbandry and health (Reh)	- 4.3.2.36
Harnessing and the use of implements (Vieberg)	- 4.3.1.62
Crop growing and ecology relevant to the use of draught animals (Lippitz)	- 4.3.1.39
Economic aspects (Munzinger)	- 4.1.34
Sociology and social anthropology (Kalb)	- 4.2.17
Case studies (Haug, Gerner-Haug)	- 4.2.13
(Smid)	- 4.2.36
(Tran Van Nhieu)	- 4.2.40
(Wagner, Munzinger)	- 4.2.42

4.3 RAMASWAMY, N.S. **Draft Report on Draught Animal Power.**
Prepared for the F.A.O. for Inter-Regional Conference on Draught Animal Power, Bangalore, 2-:6 February 1981.

Survey of the 'state of the art' of DAP for a conference sponsored by the UN Secretariat for the Conference on New and Renewable Sources of Energy. Exploratory findings are presented covering; a) The role of draught animals in development, b) The magnitude of DAP - population, distribution, value available power, c) An economic evaluation of DAP, d) The use of DAP oin farm operations - categories of use of DAP in different areas of the world, e) Animal transport and vehicles, f) Harnessing devices for all species of draught animals. g) Infrastructure for DAP - breeding, health, nutrition, subsidies, credit, implement support facilities, hiring services, slaughter and marketing, information and extension work, h) Transfer of technology - aspects of modernisation and technology levels, i) Problems and prospects of modernisation - efficiency, preference and economic aspects, j) Proposals for modernisation of DAP - institutional issues.

4.4 WATSON, P.R. **Animal Traction.** Manual No. M-12 1981, Peace Corps, Information Collection and Exchange, Appropriate Technologies for Development, 806 Connecticut Avenue, N.W., Washington D.C. 20525, U.S.A.

Practical guide to the use of draught animals and equipment written for use by workers in animal traction projects of by farmers. Discusses generally applicable principles of animal traction and provides specific information on the extension of animal powered agriculture in Africa covering; selection of power requirements, animal husbandry, nutrition, health, training procedures, yokes and harnesses, field operations and implements, with also information on economics, technical assistance and education. Included appendices cover; a) Animal power, with formulas to calculate the size of animal required for the desired amount of power, b) Animal nutrition, energy and nutrient requirements of bovines and equines, feed and feed composition, calculation of rations, recommennded rations and feeding practices, c) Disease recognition and control, d) Workshop and spare parts inventory, e) Animal traction instruction forms, f) Animal breeds used for power in Africa.

4.5 WINROCK INTERNATIONAL LIVESTOCK RESEARCH AND TRAINING CENTRE. **The Role of Ruminants in Support of Man,** Winrock International Report, April 1978, W.I.L.R.T.C., Petit Jean Mounbain, Morrilton, Arkansas, U.S.A. 72110.

Report with four broad objectives. a) To inventory on a regional basis the world population of ruminants, their output and productivity, feed requirements, the total feed resources for these ruminants and to project some of these values to 2000 AD; b) To identify the extent of the resources and the constraints to improving the level of efficiency of ruminant production, including feed resources, health problems, genetic potential, capital, market and institutional inefficiencies; c) To develop priorities for research training and development programs for ruminant livestock; d) To provide an information base for use in developing private and public investment policies for ruminant livestock and related agriculture. Report relies principally on the data bases of the F.A.O. and the grain-oilseed-livestock model of USDA's Economic Research Services.

5. CONCLUSION

A few general conclusions may be drawn from this selective review of animal draught literature.

Despite the very varied place that animal draught technologies have in small farm systems throughout the developing world, it is evident that in many situations there is scope for further developments that would lead to productivity, equity and system stability benefits over and above those presently experienced.

Where policies result in the right combination of input and output relationships, and there are suitable conditions of landholding, fodder resources and labour wage rates (eg India), animal draught technologies can play an effective and important role. It would seem to be useful to apply the lessons of this experience in areas where their current policies do not achieve government goals.

As a first step, a greater appreciation of the basis of existing technologies is essential. This would apply both from the point of view of macro level policy makers and also by research engineers, agronomists, livestock specialists and social scientists working in research and extension. There is very little analysis at present of the spontaneous spread of technologies outside the formal research and development system. In fact, important changes can occur quite rapidly and have a profound impact on the nature and productivity of systems. The spread of camel draught with locally made ploughs in Western Sudan during the past three years is a good example of such a change (J.A. Harvey personal communication).

In drawing up operational criteria for policymakers, planners, researchers and extension personnel we will start with the assumption that government goals include the need to produce food surpluses for urban populations and (where possible) export, and at the same time the government wishes to ensure that any technology that is adopted benefits the poorest members of the farming community.

For policymakers and planners the basic criteria set that could be used to decide whether a particular technology was appropriate or what conditions needed to be necessary to promote certain technologies would be:

1. Have we an adequate understanding of our existing resource base - climate, soil, livestock and human - and the way in which technology is currently generated to enable us to guide and plan future production technologies?

2. Are existing farm structures, input/output pricing systems and markets appropriate to satisfy our production and equity goals?

3. If current policies are exacerbating inequalities and suppressing the possibilities for greater equity benefits (see Baker 1982 on situation in Zambia) can they be adjusted to reverse this trend?

4. Can our production and equity goals be met without increasing our dependence on imported components, fuel and expertise?

For field level research scientists, engineers and extension workers concerned with the evolution or introduction of alternative technologies into farm systems the set of criteria is perhaps more wideranging:

1. Have we sufficient resources to diagnose farmer problems adequately and to understand the nature of present and future technology needs?

2. Given our existing institutional and operational framework, can we draw on the services and knowledge of a range of essential natural and social science personnel, including farmers, in order to evolve alternative technologies within present farming environments?

3. Have we sufficient knowledge about the likely present and future demand for technologies that are generated, either through the formal research system or independently of it?

These criteria apply equally to all types of technology, and we do not imply that animal draught based technologies, either solely or in combination with other power sources, will necessarily be superior to others. It is thought though, that had such criteria been applied, many of the past efforts at introducing new technologies may not have even started.

ANNEX 1   ORGANISATIONS WITH AN INTEREST IN PROMOTING THE USE OF DRAUGHT ANIMALS

AGRARIAN RESEARCH AND TRAINING INSTITUTE, P.O. Box 1522, 114 Wijerama Mawatha, Colombo 7, **Sri Lanka**

ASIAN INSTITUTE OF TECHNOLOGY, Bangkok, **Thailand**

C.E.E.M.A.T, Centre D'etudes et D'experimentation du Machinisme Agricole Tropical, B.P. 92160 Antony, **France**

COMMONWEALTH SECRETARIAT, Marlborough House, Pall Mall, London SW1Y 5HX, **U.K.**

CORNELL UNIVERSITY, Programme of International Agriculture, 252 Robert Hall, Cornell University, Ithaca, New York 14853, **U.S.A.**

C.T.V.M., Centre for Tropical Veterinary Medicine, Easter Bush, Roslin, Midlothian, EH25 9RG, **Scotland**

F.A.O., Food and Agriculture Organisation of the United Nations, Via Delle Terme di Caracella, 00100, Rome, **Italy**

FORD FOUNDATION, 320 East 43rd Street, New York, N.Y. 10017, **U.S.A.**

G.T.Z., Deutsche Gesellschaft fur Technische Zusammensabeit, (German Agency for Technical Cooperation), Postfach 5180, 6236 Eschborn 1, Federal Republic of **Germany**

I.C.A.R., Indian Council for Agricultural Research, Nabi Bagh, Berasia Road, Bhopal, M.P., **India**

I.I.M.- B., Indian Institute of Management, 33 Longford Road, Bangalore 560 027, **India**

I.T.D.G., Intermediate Technology Development Group, 9 King Street, London WC2E 8HN, **U.K.**

I.B.R.D., International Bank for Reconstruction and Development, (World Bank), 1818 11 Street, N.W. Washington D.C., 20433, **U.S.A.**

I.C.R.I.S.A.T., International Crops Research Institute for the Semi Arid Tropics, 1 - 11 - 256 Begumpet, Hyderabad 500016, A.P. **India**

I.L.O., International Labour Organisation, CH - 1211, Geneva 22, **Switzerland**

I.L.C.A., International Livestock Centre for Africa, P.O. Box 5689, Addis Ababa, **Ethiopia**

I.R.R.I., International Rice Research Institute, Los Banos, Laguna, **Philippines**

I.A.R., Institute of Agricultural Research, Ahmadu Bello
University, Samaru P.M.B. 1044, Zaria, **Nigeria**

I.D.S., Institute of Development Studies, University of
Nairobi, P.O. Box 30197, **Kenya**

I.D.S., Institute of Development Studies, University of
Sussex, Palmer, Brighton, BN1 9RE, **U.K.**

M.S.U. INTERNATIONAL, Michigan State University
International Development Papers, Department of
Agricultural Economics, Michigan State University, East
Lansing, Michigan 48824 - 1039,**U.S.A.**

N.I.A.E., Overseas Division, National Institute for
Agricultural Engineering, Wrest Park, Silsoe, Bedford
MK45 4HS, **U.K.**

O.D.A., Overseas Development Administration, Eland House,
Stag Place, London SW1E 5DH, **U.K.**

O.D.G., Overseas Development Group, School of Development
Studies, University of East Anglia, Norwich, NR4 7TJ,
U.K.

U.N.D.P., United Nations Development Programme, 1 United
Nations Plaza, New York 10017, **U.S.A.**

U.S.A.I.D., United States Agency for International
Development, Washington D.C., 20523, **U.S.A.**

WINROCK INTERNATIONAL, Petit Jean Mounbain, Morrilton,
Arkansas, 72110, **U.S.A.**

ANNEX 2   INDEX OF BIBLIOGRAPHY ITEMS BY AREA OR COUNTRY
               (N.B. numbers only refer to section 4, pages 10-67)

AFRICA   1.16, 1.27, 1.29, 1.33, 1.39, 1.43, 1.44, 1.45,
                1.52, 1.58;
                2.1, 2.7, 2.8, 2.19, 2.20, 2.22, 2.24, 2.31, 2.37,
                2.41, 2.50, 2.57, 2.60;
                3.1.9, 3.1.15, 3.1.22, 3.1.42;
                3.2.21, 3.2.27, 3.2.32, 3.2.49, 3.2.53, 3.2.54;
                4.2.

BANGLADESH   1.5, 1.24, 1.31, 1.42; 2.16, 2.17, 2.34, 2.39,
                2.43; 3.1.35, 3.2.40.

BOTSWANA   1.26; 3.1.20, 3.1.26, 3.1.27, 3.1.28, 3.1.29,
                3.1.34, 3.1.48, 3.1.55, 3.1.56, 3.1.72.

CAMEROON   2.38, 2.59.

CHINA   2.14; 3.2.23, 3.2.24,

ETHIOPIA   3.1.3; 3.2.11.

GAMBIA   2.33, 2.36; 3.1.16, 3.1.17, 3.1.21, 3.1.45,
                3.1.46, 3.1.58.

GHANA   2.52.

INDIA   1.10, 1.18, 1.38, 1.42, 1.47, 1.49, 1.57;
                2.5, 2.18, 2.42;
                3.1.1, 3.1.4, 3.1.8, 3.1.14, 3.1.31, 3.1.32,
                3.1.39, 3.1.40, 3.1.47, 3.1.57, 3.1.59, 3.1.60,
                3.1.61, 3.1.67, 3.1.68, 3.1.69;
                3.2.1, 3.2.3, 3.2.9, 3.2.10, 3.2.18, 3.2.31,
                3.2.37, 3.2.41, 3.2.42, 3.2.43, 3.2.44, 3.2.47,
                3.2.48, 3.2.52, 3.2.55.

INDONESIA   2.44; 3.2.57.

KENYA   1.2, 1.12, 1.46; 2.21; 3.1.37, 3.1.38, 3.1.49,
                3.1.50, 3.1.51, 3.1.52; 3.2.19.

MADAGASCAR   2.56.

MALAWI   3.1.18; 3.2.16.

MALI   2.15, 2.20; 3.1.64.

MOZAMBIQUE   2.4.

NIGERIA   1.19, 1.55; 2.30; 3.1.2, 3.1.13, 3.1.19, 3.1.53,
                3.1.54.

PAKISTAN   1.4, 1.1, 1.22, 1.41; 3.1.63; 3.2.50.

PHILIPPINES   1.7; 2.46, 2.58.

SIERRA LEONE   1.53; 2.53, 2.54; 3.1.65.

SRI LANKA	1.1, 1.20, 1.21, 1.48; 2.45; 3.2.30, 3.2.45, 3.2.56.
SUDAN	2.35; 3.1.30
SWEDEN	1.28; 3.2.21.
TANZANIA	1.30, 1.35, 1.43, 1.50, 1.51; 2.23, 2.25, 2.26, 2.32, 2.55; 3.2.35.
THAILAND	1.7.
UGANDA	1.36; 2.27, 2.40.
UNITED KINGDOM	1.23 1.56; 2.6; 3.1.5, 3.1.6, 3.1.41; 3.2.5, 3.2.6, 3.2.8, 3.2.34, 3.2.38.
UPPER VOLTA	2.3, 2.29.
ZAMBIA	1.6, 1.37, 1.54; 2.2, 2.9, 2.10, 2.13, 2.28; 3.1.23, 3.1.24.
ZIMBABWE	3.2.29.

ANNEX 3   INDEX OF BIBLIOGRAPHY ITEMS BY AUTHOR

Abeyratne, F.	1.1, 1.20, 1.21, 1.48; 2.45
Achiya, S.C.P.	3.2.1
Adelhelm, R.	1.2
Agarwal, B.	1.3
Ahmad, A.	3.2.42
Ahmad, B.	1.4
Ahmad, M.	3.2.50
Ahmad, Z.	3.2.50
Ahmed, I.	1.5
Alexander, E.N.	3.2.2
Ali, I.	3.1.1
Ali, N.	3.1.4
Aliviar, N.	1.7
Anand, U.	3.2.3
Anantharaman, S.E.	3.1.32
Anderson, F.M.	2.1
Andromedas, J.A.	3.2.4
Aremu, J.A.	3.1.2
Astatke, A.	3.1.3
Ayok, E.A.	3.1.13
Ayre, M.	3.1.7
Baker, D.	2.3, 2.8
Baker, P.R.	1.6; 2.2
Balachandran, S.S.	3.2.56
Bandara, J.	1.21
Barker, R.	1.7
Bartlett, J.	3.2.5, 3.2.6
Barrett, E.M.	3.2.5, 3.2.6

Barrett, V.	2.3
Barth, K.M.	3.2.7
Barton, D.	3.1.5, 3.1.6; 3.2.8, 3.2.34
Barwell, I.	3.1.7
Bantista, F.E.	1.8
Beeny, J.M.	1.9
Bengtsson, G.	3.2.21
Bhatagar, A.P.	3.1.68
Bhaid, M.U.	3.2.9
Bhattacharya, P.	3.2.10, 3.2.41
Bhattanagar, A.P.	3.1.68
Binswanger, H.P.	1.10; 3.1.8
Bloom, R.A.	2.50; 3.1.9
Bose, S.R.	1.11
Boshoff, W.H.	1.12; 3.1.10
Boyd, J.E.L.	1.13; 3.1.11, 3.1.12, 3.1.13
Bown, D.	3.2.11
Brodell, A.P.	3.2.12
Brown, G.D.	3.2.7
Brumby, P.J.	3.1.14
Brzeski, E	3.2.13
Buhle, P.	3.2.14
Burgemeister, R.	3.2.15
Bowmaker, R.J.	3.2.16
Carr, M.	1.14
Carson, S.P.	2.4
Castillo, L.S.	1.15
Chalmers, G.R.	3.1.15
Cham, P.	3.1.16, 3.1.17

Chitedze, F.M.I.S. - Malawi	3.1.18
Clarke, E.H.	1.11
Clarke, N.A.	2.5
Cockrill, W. Rose	3.2.17
Collinson, M.P.	1.16
Crawford, E.	2.3
Creasy, J.S.	2.6
Delago, C.L.	2.7
Dennison, J.V.	1.7
Devadattum, D.S.K.	3.2.18
Devani, R.S.	4.5.15
Dibbits, H.J.	3.2.19
Dixit, R.S.	1.18
Dunham, R.J.	1.19; 3.1.19
Dusek, j.	3.2.20
Dutta, S.	3.2.41
Dyrendahl, S.	3.2.21
E.F.S.A.I.P.	3.1.20, 3.1.21
Eicher, c.k.	2.8
Ellman, A.	3.1.22
Elmer L.A.	3.2.22
Farm Machinery Research Unit - Zambia	2.9; 3.1.23, 3.1.24
F.A.O.	2.2, 2.4, 2.5, 2.11, 2.12, 2.13, 2.17; 3.2.25, 4.1
Farrington, J.	1.20, 1.21, 1.48; 2.45
Feng Yang Lian	2.14; 3.2.23, 3.2.24
Fernsebner, R.	2.10
Finney, C.E.	1.22
Fischer, R.C.	3.1.25

Forster, J.D.G.	3.1.26
Friggins, A.R.	1.23
Froese, C.	3.1.27
Fulton, D.	2.15
Gerner-Haug, I.	2.20
Ghodake, R.D.	1.10
Gibbon, D.P.	3.16, 3.1.28, 3.1.29, 3.1.30, 3.1.34; 3.2.6, 3.2.8, 3.2.34,
Gill, B.S.	3.2.44
Gill, G.J.	1.24; 2.16
Gill, R.A.	3.2.50
Goe, M.R.	1.25; 3.2.26
Gopland, S.	3.1.31, 3.1.32
Government of Bangladesh	2.17
Government of India	2.18
Gregoive, R.	2.19
Guha, H.	3.2.52
Gupta, C.P.	3.2.30
Hall, J.F.	3.2.27
Harvey, J.A.	1.26; 3.1.29, 3.1.30, 3.1.34
Harwood, R.R.	2.46
Haswell, M.	1.27
Haug, H.	2.20
Hedman, L.	1.28
Herrera, W.A.T.	2.46
Heslop, C.	3.1.30
Heyer, J.	2.21
Honzawa, S.	3.2.28, 3.2.33
Hopfen, H.J.	3.1.33
Hossain, M.M.	3.1.35

Howard, C.R.	3.2.29
Hubbard, K.	3.1.29, 3.1.34
Humphreys, C.P.	1.29
Hussain, A.A.M.	3.1.35
Hussain, M.D.	3.1.35
Hussain, M.K.	1.42
Ilangantileke, S.G.	3.2.30
Indian Council of Agricultural Research	3.2.31
I.L.C.A.	2.22; 3.2.32
Inns, F.M.	1.30; 2.23
Ishizaki, S.	3.2.28, 3.2.33
I.T.D.G.	3.1.36
Jabbar, M.A.	1.31
James, D.P.	2.34; 3.2.40
Jayatissa, D.N.	3.2.30
Jeanrenaud, J-P.	3.1.5, 3.1.6; 3.2.8, 3.2.34
Jennings, R.D.	3.2.12
Johnson, B.F.	1.32, 1.33; 3.1.37, 3.1.38
Johnson, S.S.	1.7
Kalb, D.	2.24, 2.32
Kavishe, T.S.	3.2.35
Kaushal, M.P.	3.1.40
Kemp, D.C.	3.1.39
Ker, A.D.P.	1.34
Khepar, S.D.	3.1.40
Kinsey, B.H.	1.35, 1.36, 1.37; 2.26, 2.27, 2.28
Kiyama, K.	3.2.28
Kjaerby, P.	2.25
Knierim, S.C.	3.1.47

Koyama, K.	3.2.28, 3.2.33
Krautforst, J.W.	3.2.36
Kumar, A.	3.1.69
Kumdu, P.B.	1.38
Lall, H.K.	3.2.37
Lassiter, G.	2.3, 2.29
Laurent, C.K.	2.30
Lawrence, P.	3.1.41
Lele, U.	1.39
Le Moigne, M.	2.31
Lewis, R.E.	3.2.4
Lichte, J.A.	2.50
Link, H.	2.32
Lippitz, K.	3.1.42
Lockerltz, F.C.	1.40
Lowe, P.	3.1.43
McDowell, R.E.	3.2.26, 3.2.39
McIntire, R.E.	2.7
Mackay, B.	3.1.22, 3.1.44
Marsden, R.H.	3.1.15
Masud, S.W.	1.41
Mathers, J.C.	3.2.38
Matlon, P.J.	2.50
Matthews, M.D.P.	3.1.3, 3.1.45, 3.1.46
Maurya, N.L.	3.2.18
Mettrick, H.	2.33, 2.34; 3.2.40
Mian, M.S.J.	1.42
Michael, A.M.	3.1.47
Ministry of Finance - Sudan	2.35

Minto, S.D.	1.12, 1.43; 3.1.10
Mishra, T.N.	3.1.69
Mochudi Farmers' Brigade	3.1.48
Moczarski, S.Z.	2.36
Moody, T.	3.1.22
Morstin, J.	3.2.13
Muchiri, G.	1.43; 3.1.37, 3.1.38, 3.1.49, 3.1.50, 3.1.51
Muckle, B.	3.1.52
Mukherjee, M.	3.2.41
Mukolwe, M.	3.1.52
Munzinger, P.	1.44; 2.37, 2.59; 4.2
Musa, H.L.	3.1.53
Nangia, O.P.	3.2.42
Nell, A.J.	2.44
Nugi, A.K.	3.2.52
Neunhauser, P.	2.38
Norman, D.	3.2.51
Odend'Hal, S.	2.39
Ogborn, J.E.A.	3.1.54
Okai, M.	2.40
Oloufa, M.M.	1.45
Orciono, N.	1.7
Orev, Y.	2.41; 3.1.55, 3.1.56
Pathak, B.S.	3.1.57; 3.2.43, 3.2.44
Patra, S.K.	3.1.4
Paul, C.V.	3.1.59
Peacock, J.M.	3.1.58
Pearson, S.R.	1.29
Perdok, H.B.	3.2.45

Peter, E.C.	3.1.59
Pollard, S.J.	1.46
Pullen, D.W.M.	3.1.45, 3.1.46
Ranaswamy, N.S.	3.1.60; 3.2.46, 4.3
Rana, R.D.	3.2.42
Rao, A.R.	2.42
Rao, M.V.M.	3.2.47
Rao, P.S.	3.1.61
Rant, K.C.	3.2.48
Reddy, C.V.	1.47
Reeser, R.M.	3.1.47
Reh, I.	3.2.49
Richards, J.I.	2.43
Rizwan-ul-Muqtadir	3.2.50
Roesyak, A.	3.2.57
Rollinson, D.H.L.	2.44
Roth, M.	3.2.51
Roy, S.R.	3.2.52
Ryan, J.G.	1.57
Ryan, M.J.	1.21, 1.48; 2.45
Smason, B.T.	2.46
Sargent, M.W.	2.47, 2.48, 2.49, 2.50
Sasimowski, E.	3.2.53, 3.2.54
Schmidt, H.	1.2
Schutjer, W.A.	2.51
Scott, D.	3.1.62
Scott, M.	3.2.11
Seager, A.	3.1.63
Sharma, R.K.	1.49
Shinihara, A.	3.2.28, 3.2.33

Schulman, R.	3.1.64
Singh, B.K.	3.2.55
Singh, D.	3.2.55
Singh, I.	1.50, 1.51; 2.42
Singh, K.	3.1.14
Singh, M.	3.1.40
Singh, N.	3.2.42
Singh, R.K.	3.2.55
Singh, R.P.	3.1.69
Siriwardene, J.A.	3.2.56
Sitorus, P.	3.2.57
Sleeper, J.A.	1.52
Smid, J.	2.52
Smith, A.J.	3.2.58, 3.2.59, 3.2.60
Starkey, P.	1.53; 2.53, 2.54; 3.1.65
Stocking, M.	1.54
Stokes, A.R.	1.55
Strachan, G.	1.56
Subramanium, J.	1.51
Subramanium, K.V.	1.57
Sundaeasen, D.	3.2.3
Sutherland, T.M.	1.59
Swamy Rao, A.A.	3.1.66, 3.1.67
T.I.R.D.E.P.	2.55
Telleen, M.	3.2.61
Thierstein, G.E.	1.10, 1.58; 3.1.8
Tornede, H.	3.2.62
Toulmin, D.	2.15
Tran Van Nhien, J.	2.56

Twk, K.L.	3.2.63
Underwood, F.L.	1.41
Uzurean, C.	2.57
Undundo, G.	3.2.1
Van der Veen, M.G.	2.51
Varma, S.R.	3.1.68
Varshney, B.P.	3.1.69
Verhaeghe, H.	1.53; 3.1.65
Viebig, V.	3.1.70
Villegar, V.	2.58
Wagner, C.M.	2.59
Wainaina, C.K.	1.46
Wallis, M.	1.23
Ward, G.M.	1.59
Watson, P.R.	4.4
White, P.	1.6
Wickham, T.	1.8
Wickremasuriya, U.	3.2.56
Wilcock, D.	2.3
Willcocks T.J.	3.1.71, 3.1.72
Williams, J.W.	3.2.7
Winrock International L.R.T.C.	4.
Wright, D.	2.60
Zulbardi, M.	3.2.57

www.ingramcontent.com/pod-product-compliance
Ingram Content Group UK Ltd.
Pitfield, Milton Keynes, MK11 3LW, UK
UKHW060455150426
5217IPUK00028B/2084